ROY DOUGLAS is Emeritus Reader at the University of Surrey. He is author of a number of historical books. These include four books of international cartoons covering between them the period 1848–1945; a history of the Liberal Party; a study of the Land Question in UK politics; and five books on twentieth-century diplomatic history. He has almost completed a history of taxation since 1660. He was on five occasions a Liberal parliamentary candidate, and is active in the land reform movement.

LIAM HARTE was born in County Mayo and graduated from University College Galway with a degree in English and Modern History. He holds a doctorate from Trinity College Dublin and is Senior Lecturer in Irish Studies at St Mary's University College, Strawberry Hill. He has published several journal articles on modern Irish literature and is the contributing co-editor of *Contemporary Irish Fiction: Themes, Tropes, Theories* (Macmillan, 1999). He is currently compiling an anthology of autobiographical prose by the Irish in Britain.

JIM O'HARA was born in Belfast. He graduated from Queen's University Belfast and was later awarded an MA in Modern History at Queen Mary College, London University. He has been a history lecturer in various universities in Britain, and in 1990 established the Irish Studies Centre at St Mary's University College. A founder member of the British Association for Irish Studies as well as the European Federation of Centres for Irish Studies, he also chairs the Advisory Committee of the Irish Youth Federation in the United Kingdom and is a member of the Irish Government's DION committee. His articles and reviews have been published in *Irish Studies*, *Fortnight*, *Ouest-France* and *Éire-Ireland*, and he contributed to *All Ireland* (New Burlington Books, 1988).

Jim O'Hara currently lives in Richmond, Surrey, and is Principal Lecturer in Irish Studies at St Mary's University College, Strawberry Hill.

Roy Douglas, Liam Harte and Jim O'Hara are the co-authors of *Drawing Conclusions: A Cartoon History of Anglo-Irish Relations, 1798–1998* (Blackstaff Press, 1998).

Ireland
since 1690
A CONCISE HISTORY

ROY DOUGLAS • LIAM HARTE • JIM O'HARA

CONTEMPORARY BOOKS

Library of Congress Cataloging-in-Publication Data

Douglas, Roy, 1924–
     Ireland since 1690 : a concise history / Roy Douglas, Liam Harte, Jim O'Hara.
         p.   cm.
     Rev. and fully updated text based on Drawing conclusions by the same authors.
     Includes index.
     ISBN 0-8092-9898-8
     1. Ireland—History—1690–   .   I. Harte, Liam.   II. O'Hara, Jim.   III. Douglas, Roy, 1924–   . Drawing conclusions.   IV. Title.
DA938.D68   2000
941.508—dc21   00-35842

First published in 1999 by The Blackstaff Press Limited, Blackstaff House, Wildflower Way, Apollo Road, Belfast BT12 6TA, Northern Ireland.

This revised and fully updated text is based on that of *Drawing Conclusions: A Cartoon History of Anglo-Irish Relations, 1798–1998* (1998) by the same authors.

Cover painting: *Siege II* by Rita Duffy
Typesetting by Techniset Typesetters, Newton-le-Willows, Merseyside

This edition first published in 2000 in the United States by
Contemporary Books
A division of NTC/Contemporary Publishing Group, Inc.
4255 West Touhy Avenue
Lincolnwood (Chicago), Illinois 60712-1975 U.S.A.
Printed in England by Biddles Limited
International Standard Book Number: 0-8092-9898-8
00 01 02 03 04 05   15 14 13 12 11 10 9 8 7 6 5 4 3 2 1

To our students
at St Mary's University College
and the University of Surrey

While all the historians make mention of the large states if they have fulfilled any noble achievement, it seems to me that if a state which is small has accomplished many noble deeds, it is even more fitting to set them forth.

XENOPHON, *Hellenica* VII. 2. 1.

CONTENTS

1

CONQUEST AND ASCENDANCY
1690–1775

Few dates in the history of Ireland have such resonance as 1690, the year in which King William of Orange (1650–1702), a Dutch Protestant, won a crucial victory over the Catholic King James II (1633–1701) at the Battle of the Boyne. This Williamite success, which was followed by another important military victory at the Battle of Aughrim in 1691, marked the decisive defeat of Catholicism as a political force in Ireland and laid the foundations for almost two centuries of Protestant rule. During this period the country was governed by a small landowning class known as the Protestant ascendancy, amounting to no more than five thousand families, in whose hands power, wealth and privilege were concentrated. The members of this governing class were descended from English colonists of the sixteenth century and adhered to the established Church of Ireland, a body in full communion with the Church of England and the official religion of the state. At a cultural level, the events of 1690–91 shaped the identity and outlook of subsequent generations of Irish Protestants and Catholics and supplied them with an enduring iconography of siege and deliverance, fortitude and triumph, dispossession and oppression. Over three hundred years later, the political and cultural ramifications of these events are still detectable in Irish life, especially in the divisions within Northern Ireland. To understand the reasons for this, it is necessary to examine the historical factors which led to this epic confrontation, which was in essence a struggle between a newly emerged Protestant élite and a once powerful Catholic community.

For over a century prior to 1690, Ireland had been the site of a fierce struggle between the forces of the Protestant Reformation, inaugurated by the Tudor state in the 1530s and backed by successive English governments, and the Catholic Counter-Reformation, supported by most of the native Gaelic Irish aristocracy and the Old English community, made up of descendants of the twelfth-century Anglo-Norman conquerors. The origins of the Anglo-Irish conflict are much older than the Reformation, however, and are political rather than religious in character. A long, complex power struggle between English and Irish élites had been taking place since 1169, the year in which Anglo-Norman feudal lords first invaded Ireland. Although English political control had been achieved by the early seventeenth century, the religious division between a Protestant state and an overwhelmingly Catholic people remained a fundamental problem of Irish government.

Under King James I, the Tudor policy of piecemeal plantation, whereby loyal Protestant settlers were granted the confiscated estates of rebellious Catholics, became the preferred official solution. However, the plantation of Ulster, which began in 1609, served only to exacerbate the religious antagonism between native and settler. The plantation fundamentally altered the character of the province, establishing large areas in which the mass of the population was either English or Scottish in origin, and adhered either to the established Church of England or to the Scottish Presbyterian Church. The systematic granting of land to these Protestant 'undertakers', so called because they undertook to defend English authority, religion and 'civility' in Ireland, caused festering resentment among the dispossessed Catholics, many of whom were driven into the bogs and woodlands, though some ended up holding tenancies under the new dispensation.

Native resentment erupted into violence in 1641, when Catholics in Ulster attacked their settler neighbours, prompting greatly exaggerated tales of the massacre of Protestants. The fact that the rising occurred on the eve of the English civil wars between King Charles I and the Protestant parliament meant that it was several years before an English expeditionary force could be raised to suppress the rebellion, which soon spread to other parts of Ireland. In August 1649 Oliver Cromwell (1599–1658), the newly installed head of the English Commonwealth, arrived in Ireland with a twenty-thousand-strong army backed up by a large naval force. Over the next nine months he carried out a brutal campaign of suppression against Catholics and royalists, including bloody massacres at Drogheda and Wexford, the ruthlessness of which led to his demonisation as an arch-villain in Irish folk memory. The Cromwellian conquest was quickly followed by an equally punitive land settlement scheme, whereby English soldiers and adventurers were given the confiscated lands of disloyal Catholics.

By 1660, therefore, the date of the restoration of the monarchy under the Stuart King Charles II, Catholic political power in Ireland was effectively at an end. Land, the source of wealth and the basis of power, was heavily concentrated in Protestant hands. Membership of the Irish parliament was also Protestant dominated, as was the control and exercise of municipal power. Two decades later, however, hopes of a Catholic revival were rekindled when James II succeeded to the English throne on the death of his brother, Charles II, in 1685. The new king's avowed commitment to reviving Catholicism delighted Irish Catholics, who believed that the restoration of their faith and the recovery of their lands were at hand. These hopes were boosted when James appointed a leading advocate of Catholic claims, Richard Talbot, Earl of Tyrconnell, head of the Irish army, and subsequently made him viceroy, the first Catholic to hold this position for over one hundred years. Tyrconnell's elevation was followed by the appointment of increasing numbers of Irish Catholics to positions of administrative, judicial and military power, bringing the possibility of a reversal of the Cromwellian settlement ever closer. But while Catholics rejoiced at this prospect, it greatly alarmed Irish Protestants, and raised grave fears in England of what might be expected from a popish king.

Matters came to a head following the birth of a son and heir to James in June 1688. The prospect of the foundation of a Catholic royal dynasty prompted English magnates to offer the throne to Prince William of Orange, husband of James's Protestant daughter, Mary. When William arrived in England in November 1688 with fourteen thousand troops, the king's cause collapsed and James fled to France, where he established a court-in-exile with the backing of King Louis XIV. His departure allowed William to assume power and set in motion a series of constitutional changes known as the Glorious Revolution, which provided the basis for the Protestant succession to the English throne. But while the revolution itself had been a bloodless one, it had bloody consequences, especially in Ireland, which became a major theatre of European war in 1689–90.

One of William's chief motives for intervening in English affairs was to secure English aid for his campaign to prevent Louis xiv from dominating Europe. Similarly, Louis's support for James's attempt to recapture his throne was motivated by his desire to defeat his enemies in Europe. Thus, when James arrived in Ireland in March 1689 with French soldiers and supplies, hoping to use the country as a base from which to regain his crown, Ireland became directly involved in a complex international conflict. The 'war of the two kings', as it was known in Gaelic, was important within a number of political contexts, therefore. In the immediate Irish context, it was a struggle for religious and political supremacy between two élites; in a British context, it was a battle of royal succession; whereas in a wider European context, it was a strategic phase in a war of territorial expansion. For the two kings, the British and European dimensions took primacy; for their respective Irish supporters, the political destiny of their country mattered most.

The hour of reckoning was not yet at hand, however. For much of 1689, William's attention remained focused on the Continent, following his declaration of war on France as part of a Grand Alliance, which included the United Provinces, Spain and the Holy Roman Empire. In Ireland, meanwhile, the Jacobite army laid siege to Derry, where they were met with cries of 'no surrender!' and armed resistance from the Protestant inhabitants. After a fifteen-week ordeal during which thousands died from disease and starvation, the siege was lifted. To many, then and since, the event epitomised the unbreakable spirit of Protestant fortitude and is still celebrated in the annual parades of the Derry Apprentice Boys, a Protestant political society named after the thirteen apprentices who shut the city gates against the Jacobite troops in December 1688.

Despite the successful Protestant defence of Derry, and other, less spectacular, victories by the Enniskillen Protestants, Jacobite morale remained high, boosted by the arrival of additional French troops in March 1690. William responded by sending Dutch reinforcements, before taking personal charge of his army in June. The key battle, the most famous in Irish history, occurred on 1 July, when the armies of the two kings met at the River Boyne near Drogheda in County Louth. (The change from the Julian to the Gregorian calendar in 1752 meant that the annual commemoration of the battle henceforth took place on 12 July.) William's victory was seen in Europe as a major defeat for Louis xiv and was celebrated in the Catholic cathedrals of William's allies, Spain and Austria. It was also welcomed by the Pope, an irony made all the richer by the subsequent history of religious conflict in Ireland.

Within Ireland itself, however, the battle was less decisive. Irish losses were small, and although James fled to France, most of the Jacobite forces escaped to fight for another year, inspired by their Irish commander, Patrick Sarsfield. The ensuing departure of the French troops left a predominantly Irish Jacobite army in the field, its members now fighting for themselves and their civil and religious liberties rather than for James. They were finally defeated at the Battle of Aughrim in County Galway on 12 July 1691, the last pitched battle to be fought on Irish soil, and probably the bloodiest, with as many as seven thousand Irishmen slaughtered in the field. With the capture of Limerick by Williamite forces a few months later, Jacobite resistance collapsed.

The 1691 treaty of Limerick which ended the Williamite War was not ungenerous to the vanquished. Although confiscation of land took place, it was much less than that seized after the Cromwellian conquest. In fact, the treaty allowed numerous former Catholic rebels to keep their land and property.

Moreover, Catholics were guaranteed the same religious rights as they had enjoyed during Charles II's reign and were allowed to practise their trades and professions, though loose drafting and the omission of important clauses in the final version left the specific terms of the treaty dangerously open to future interpretation. The surrendering Jacobite soldiers were given the option of going to France, where they could continue to fight in the armies of France, Spain and Austria. Within ten weeks of the treaty being signed, Sarsfield led some twelve thousand Irish troops, many with wives and children, into exile. This exodus of the greater part of the Catholic gentry, which became known as 'the flight of the Wild Geese', meant that Irish regiments formed a distinctive part of the mainly Catholic armies of France and Spain during the eighteenth century, earning special fame for their contribution to the French victory over the British at the Battle of Fontenoy in 1745. This expatriate community also forged links with the many Irish Catholic seminaries on the Continent, creating an informal network which made a unique and valued contribution to European culture.

Irish Protestants, however, were deeply dissatisfied with the terms of the treaty of Limerick relating to land and religion, believing them to be much too generous to Catholics. Having regained their ascendancy after a bitter struggle, they were determined to preserve their security by ensuring that their enemies would never again be in a position to gain power. As a result, the toleration of Catholics promised in the treaty was not honoured, and when, in 1691, the English parliament passed an act making it impossible for Catholics to become MPs, Irish Protestants seized the opportunity to consolidate their ascendancy in all aspects of Irish life. From 1692 until its abolition in 1800, the Irish parliament would be dominated by the Protestant propertied interest.

The chief means by which Irish Protestants maintained their political stranglehold during this period was through the enactment of a series of 'popery' or 'penal laws', introduced between 1695 and 1729. These were designed to curtail the political, economic and religious freedoms of Catholics, who comprised about 75 per cent of the population, and, to a lesser extent, of Presbyterians and other non-Anglicans, collectively known as Dissenters. The laws severely restricted the rights of Catholics to practise their faith, receive an education, hold public office, bear arms, vote, sit in parliament, possess a horse worth more than five pounds and, above all, buy, lease or inherit land.

Control of land was the key to the Protestant ascendancy. Catholics were forbidden to lease land for more than thirty-one years and on the death of a Catholic landowner, his property had to be divided equally among his sons, thereby ensuring a decline in the family's wealth and status. If, however, an eldest son converted to the established Church of Ireland on or before his father's death, the entire property became his. Though not all these statutes were fully enforced, this punitive land legislation drastically reduced the proportion of Catholic landownership, which declined from 22 per cent in 1688 to around 14 per cent by the end of the century. By 1775, land ownership among Catholics had fallen to about 5 per cent, thereby swelling the ranks of the Catholic poor, described by George Townshend, the Irish lord lieutenant in 1770, as 'amongst the most wretched people on earth'.

The penal laws were aimed primarily at the Irish Catholic élite, the gentry who had been the traditional leaders of their people. Such legislation was not confined to Ireland; in France, Spain and the Holy Roman Empire, discriminatory laws existed against religious minorities such as Protestants and Jews. What made the Irish situation unique, however, was the fact that these laws victimised the majority Catholic population. Penal legislation also affected the third religious grouping on the island, the Protestant Dissenters, most of whom were of Scottish Presbyterian origin. These were solidly grouped in north-east Ulster, where their hard-headed, independent-minded outlook made them a distinctive and formidable bloc. They too were excluded from public office and, in turn, resented the dominance of the Church of Ireland ascendancy class. During the eighteenth century considerable numbers of Presbyterians left Ulster to seek a more tolerant environment in the American colonies. Some of these emigrants later became prominent in asserting their rights against Britain during the American War of Independence of the 1770s. Two decades later, Presbyterian radicals in Ulster, inspired by the ideals of the French Revolution, sought to emulate the example of their American cousins by making common cause with Catholic and Protestant republicans in the movement of the United Irishmen.

Among the Catholic masses, one notable feature of the penal law era was the forging of a strong bond between the people and the priesthood at a popular level. Although the discriminatory religious restrictions fell into disuse from about 1716, Catholics continued to regard their religion and their Church as alternative sources of authority and allegiance to that represented by the politicians and landlords of the Anglo-Irish ascendancy. For many Catholics, the priest, usually a man of similar background and outlook to themselves, acted as leader and adviser in both spiritual and material affairs. Later, in the nineteenth century, the latent political potential of this affiliation between clergy and laity was strategically exploited by Daniel O'Connell, whose campaign for Catholic emancipation united priests and people in a powerful national alliance.

The vast majority of the population of eighteenth-century

Ireland consisted of impoverished Gaelic-speaking peasants. These were either cottiers living with their animals in tiny cabins, renting little plots of land, or landless labourers, the most economically disadvantaged peasant group. Throughout the century, the legal and social persecution under which the Catholic peasantry laboured was exacerbated by the exploitative activities of rapacious landlords. Many Irish landlords were absentees who delegated control of their estates to agents or middlemen, whose overriding concern was to extract the maximum amount of rent possible in the short term. Such people had little interest in the welfare of their tenant-farmers, most of whom lacked any incentive to carry out improvements to their holdings.

The precarious existence of the rural poor was worsened by their increasing dependency on the potato and the consequent risk of famine if the crop failed. Famine was endemic in Ireland, as harvests were frequently erratic and poor weather could cause serious food shortages. The years 1739–41 witnessed famine on an unprecedented scale. A harsh and prolonged frost during the winter of 1739–40 destroyed most of the potato crop, and the return of frosty weather in the autumn of 1741 led to a huge famine disaster. While the uneven impact of the disaster led to regional variations in the death rate, it is generally accepted that approximately one-eighth of Ireland's population died from hunger or disease in these years, proportionately as many as were to die in the better-remembered famine of the 1840s. After 1741 there were no severe food shortages for several decades and the population increased steadily, probably doubling to almost five million by 1800.

This increase in population was paralleled by a period of economic growth, as the linen industry developed rapidly in the north and the agricultural sector expanded to meet a growing demand for provisions. While the poorer classes benefited from this economic upturn, it was the propertied gentry which displayed its increased wealth with enduring architectural grandeur. By 1750, the first of the great country houses of Georgian Ireland had been built. These magnificent mansions, built in the style of the English aristocracy, complete with their elaborate parks and gardens, bore witness to the ostentatious confidence of the Protestant landowning class. Having achieved victory over its religious rivals and demonstrated its political potency to its colonial masters, the Protestant ascendancy sought social and cultural prestige. Thus, Dublin became the second city of the British Isles and the centre of a vibrant social scene during the parliamentary season. Architecturally, it became one of the finest capitals of Europe, with its spacious squares, elegant houses, wide streets and splendid public buildings such as the Custom House and the Four Courts. The completion of a magnificent Parliament House at College Green in 1731, looking out on a renovated Trinity College, was perhaps the ultimate expression of Anglo-Irish supremacy, Protestant parliament now complementing Protestant university.

Despite the general improvement in Ireland's economy, the abject condition of the peasantry deteriorated further from mid-century, when the rise in population intensified the competition for land. This led to a growth in agrarian unrest which manifested itself in the formation of secret societies with names like the Whiteboys in Munster and the Hearts of Oak in Ulster, groups dedicated to seeking summary redress for the local grievances of the poor by means of intimidation and violence. Bands of armed peasants regularly carried out nocturnal attacks against landlords' property and livestock, the chief targets of their protests being the shift from tillage to pasture, which often led to the enclosure of common land for grazing, the imposition of high rents, and the payment of the much-resented tithe, at a time when many lived barely above starvation level. The tithe was a compulsory annual tax levied on Catholics and Dissenters, as well as on members of the established Church, for the upkeep of the Church of Ireland. Although these grievances were local and particular, Protestant fears of Whiteboy activity led to the first of several acts being passed against them in 1766. However, such coercive measures served only to reinforce the anti-authoritarian attitudes of the peasant masses and confirm their lack of faith in the legal system to redress their grievances. As a result, secret oath-bound societies continued to exist well into the latter half of the nineteenth century and it was to these groups that many peasants turned for protection in times of extreme distress, rather than to the law of the land.

For all their subversive potential, the political horizons of such groups were narrowly parochial and they lacked any wider national aims or objectives. In Ulster, however, agrarian violence assumed an increasingly sectarian complexion in the closing decades of the century, as competition for land intensified because of a population increase, and relief acts gave Catholics greater freedom to bid for leases. Catholic peasants formed themselves into a Defender organisation to protect themselves against dawn attacks from the Peep o' Day Boys, a Protestant secret society. These groups fought each other in bloody pitched battles, often in broad daylight, thereby beginning a tradition of bitter sectarian animosity that was to continue into the late twentieth century. This rivalry reached an early climax in 1795 at the Battle of the Diamond in County Armagh, when the Peep o' Day Boys defeated the Defenders and left about thirty of them dead. After this brutal confrontation, the Protestant forces reconstituted themselves as the Orange Order, named after their deliverer of 1690, and dedicated themselves to the defence of Protestant supremacy over Catholics. This development was to have profound importance for the subsequent history of Ulster and the Orange Order remains a formidable force in the politics of contemporary Northern Ireland.

The Anglo-Irish relationship in the eighteenth century was quintessentially a colonial one. However much the Anglican ascendancy resented this fact, it realised that as a vulnerable and isolated minority surrounded by a potentially hostile Catholic majority, it was dependent upon the military strength of the mother country to protect and maintain its privileged position. Although Ireland had its own parliament, its powers were severely curtailed by Westminster under a fifteenth-century statute known as Poynings's Law, which prescribed that no legislative initiative should be taken in Ireland without the authority of the English king and privy council. From the early 1690s, however, the Irish parliament established itself as a key factor in the government of Ireland. This came about as a result of a financial crisis caused by Britain's need to raise revenue in Ireland in the aftermath of its very costly war against James II and the French. By insisting on control of taxation, the Irish parliament asserted its right to initiate financial legislation and guaranteed that it would have to meet on a regular basis if the government was to obtain the revenues it required. The Irish Commons' subsequent enactment of the penal laws against Catholics and Dissenters confirmed its ability to assert its primacy in internal affairs.

This assertion of parliamentary control was part of a wider sense of Anglo-Irish Protestant resentment at what they saw as their unequal treatment by Britain, which meant that the period between 1691 and 1725 was one of constant friction between London and Dublin. Their grievances were of three main kinds. At a constitutional level, they resented the claim of the British parliament to pass legislation binding on Ireland, and that of the British House of Lords to act as the final court of appeal in Ireland. From an economic perspective, they objected to Ireland's commerce and trade being restrictively regulated in the interests of the imperial power, as evidenced by the 1699 Woollen Act, which banned the export of Irish woollen goods to any country other than England, as the cheaper Irish materials were undercutting English goods in overseas markets. In addition, the Anglo-Irish élite resented the large numbers of British appointees to important positions within the Irish civil, military and religious establishments.

Of these three grievances, it was the constitutional one which caused most discontent among Irish Protestants. When the legislative supremacy of the British parliament was enshrined in the 1720 Declaratory Act, 'an act for the better securing of the dependency of the Kingdom of Ireland upon the Crown of Great Britain', it seemed that Britain now controlled Ireland's political and economic destiny. The perception from London was that Ireland was a conquered country which the Protestant ascendancy, acting as a kind of colonial garrison, had a duty to maintain and administer on behalf of the crown. Irish Protestants countered this view, firstly, by appealing to the historic right of Ireland to be considered as a separate kingdom, and secondly, by arguing that all men had a right to be represented in the parliament which governed them.

This latter argument, which was rooted in a concept of universal human rights, was most clearly articulated in a pamphlet written in 1698 by William Molyneux, a friend of the English philosopher John Locke. Molyneux's tract, which was widely reprinted in the eighteenth century, advocated 'government by consent' and defended the autonomy of the Irish parliament. His arguments had a profound influence on English radicals, American colonists and Irish 'patriots', an opposition faction within the Protestant propertied class. While these patriots were not arguing for independence in a national sense, the Anglo-Irish Protestant community's continuing resentment at British economic exploitation combined with a growing sense of its cultural distinctiveness to produce a demand for parliamentary autonomy as the century unfolded.

In the 1720s Jonathan Swift (1667–1745), dean of St Patrick's Cathedral in Dublin, emerged as one of the most eloquent advocates of this Protestant Irish 'nationalism'. Speaking on behalf of what he termed 'the whole people of Ireland' (in fact, the Protestant colonial élite), he wrote a series of brilliant political pamphlets in which he savagely attacked Britain's maltreatment of the country and angrily rejected the right of the Westminster parliament to legislate for Ireland. Hailed as the first Hibernian patriot, it was Swift who coined the slogan 'burn everything English except their coal!', a nationalist catchphrase which has echoed down the centuries. His pamphlet series, *The Drapier's Letters* (1724–25), played a key role in uniting Irish Protestant resistance to George I's attempt to grant a patent for the minting of copper coinage for Ireland to the advantage of his German ex-mistress, the so-called Wood's halfpence controversy. In 1729 his most devastating political essay, *A Modest Proposal*, bitterly satirised England's indifference to the death and suffering caused by three years of famine in Ireland. In this he ironically suggests that young children be fattened and slaughtered as 'a most delicious, nourishing, and wholesome food . . . for landlords, who, as they have already devoured most of the parents, seem to have the best title to the children'.

In these and other works Swift voiced the sentiments of most Irish Protestants when he argued that Ireland was a sister kingdom to England and her equal under the crown. However, he and his fellow colonial nationalists were careful to distinguish between their opposition to the British parliament and their loyalty to the British crown. Their claim to be treated as an equal nation was based on the argument that as descendents of English settlers in Ireland they were entitled to the same rights as their fellow subjects in England, and that these rights were being denied them by an interfering British parliament. In short, they saw themselves as Irishmen with English civil rights. Thus, the desire for legislative independence was entirely compatible with loyalty to monarchical government in the minds of the eighteenth-century Irish Protestant. However, as the century progressed and Protestants came to identify more strongly with Ireland, many also began to place greater emphasis on the idea of parliamentary independence.

A series of political and economic conflicts between Britain and Ireland in the period 1691–1725 led British ministers to conclude that Ireland could not be governed effectively without the active co-operation of the powerful Protestant minority. After the 1720s, therefore, London only infrequently exercised its powers to interfere with Irish parliamentary legislation, and made very sparing use of its rights to pass laws for Ireland. But the need remained for Britain to control and manage an Irish parliament that was growing in importance and becoming increasingly independent in financial affairs. The fact that successive lord lieutenants – English politicians who were appointed head of the Irish administration – were usually unfamiliar with Ireland, and resided there on a temporary basis only, made this need all the more pressing.

For much of the eighteenth century, therefore, the government relied on 'undertakers' to maintain parliamentary control. These were local politicians who undertook to secure majorities for government measures in the Irish parliament, especially on the all-important finance bills, in return for a substantial share of government patronage for themselves and their followers. In practice, therefore, parliamentary control was vested in the hands of a small number of rich and powerful undertakers such as William Conolly and Henry Boyle, who operated an effective, if unedifying, political system with which the ascendancy class was largely content. A comparatively small number of Irish landowners controlled a majority of the parliamentary seats, restrictive property qualifications ensuring that only a small proportion of people had the vote, and the absence of a secret ballot meant that many voters were vulnerable to landlord influence. The additional fact that Catholics were denied the franchise for most of the century meant that parliament was in no real sense representative. Yet despite these impediments, parliament could still give expression to a form of Protestant nationalism, and in the years after 1760 the patriot tradition established by Molyneux and Swift was to enjoy a spectacular revival.

The attitude of government to the undertaker system was to change, however, especially in the wake of the money bill dispute of the 1750s, when Boyle spearheaded Irish parliamentary opposition to a British attempt to appropriate surplus revenue from the Irish Exchequer. Westminster responded by appointing a permanently resident lord lieutenant, George Townshend, in 1767. He set about depriving the undertakers of their lucrative position by dispensing patronage himself from his power base in Dublin Castle. In this way he built up an informal 'Castle party', a body of supporters in parliament upon which he could depend to pass legislation.

The emergence of this parliamentary grouping contributed to the growth of the opposition patriots, a loose body of MPs led initially by Henry Flood (1732–91). Although in no sense an organised party, the patriots had a shared aim of freeing Ireland from the economic and political restrictions placed upon it by Britain. In particular, they challenged British policy makers' view of Ireland as a dependent colony and refused to accept that the Dublin parliament was subject to the legislative authority of Westminster. As well as aiming to secure Irish colonial independence, Flood supported the removal of the penal religious restrictions on Catholics, but opposed admitting them to the political nation, realising that this would spell the end of Protestant supremacy. In 1775 Henry Grattan (1746–1820), the most famous eighteenth-century Irish patriot leader, joined Flood in parliament. He envisaged an independent Irish parliament under the crown in a new nation of Protestants and Catholics, arguing that 'the Irish Protestant could never be free till the Irish Catholic had ceased to be a slave'. These two issues – the nature of Ireland's relationship with Britain and the rights of Irish Catholics – which had continually troubled the relative calm of the eighteenth century, were about to force themselves onto the Anglo-Irish political agenda with renewed insistence in the closing decades of the century.

2

REBELLION AND UNION
1776–1800

The American War of Independence which began in 1775 had a profound influence on Irish politics, not least because there were significant similarities between the position of Ireland and that of the American colonies within the British imperial framework. Discontented Anglo-Irishmen readily identified with the political aspirations of the colonists, many of whom were Ulster Presbyterian immigrants, frustrated by their exclusion from active citizenship in Ireland by the harsh penal code. However, the Irish response to the American revolt was somewhat ambiguous in that sympathy for the rebels was counterbalanced by fear of invasion by enemies closer to home. When France and Spain sought to exploit Britain's transatlantic difficulties by entering the war on the American side in 1778–79, Ireland lay open to invasion, as most regular troops had been redeployed in America. In their absence, Irish Protestants rallied to defend the country against an opportunistic attack.

Starting in Ulster in 1778, they began forming themselves into companies of armed Volunteers – the eighteenth-century equivalent of a paramilitary group – which by 1780 contained over forty thousand men. Of course, such a formidable show of defensive strength also had enormous offensive potential, particularly if used to exact constitutional concessions from a vulnerable British government. This recognition led the parliamentary leaders of the Volunteer movement, Flood and Grattan, to exploit this popular extra-parliamentary pressure group, which was outside the control of government, to push for economic and political reforms, including legislative independence. Although the Volunteers were made up of respectable middle-class Protestants, well-disciplined by upper-class officers, the government feared the potential threat they posed to the rule of law.

A worried British administration considered it expedient, therefore, to conciliate the Catholic majority in case of invasion or internal strife, and so in 1778 a Relief Act was passed, allowing Catholics to lease and inherit land on the same terms as other religious denominations. The following year, Volunteer support for Grattan's patriot party forced the government to lift its restrictions on Irish trade. Grattan's finest hour came in 1782, when he succeeded in winning legislative independence from a British government weakened by its defeat at the hands of the American colonists. His Declaration of Independence was unanimously accepted by the Irish Commons, forcing the British parliament to amend Poynings's Law and repeal the Declaratory Act. The following year, Westminster specifically renounced its claim to legislate for Ireland. Thus began eighteen years of partial Irish parliamentary autonomy (1782–1800), known to history as the era of Grattan's parliament.

The independence of the Irish parliament was more nominal than real, however, because of its corrupt and unrepresentative nature. In a political culture where parliamentary seats were openly bought and sold, two-thirds of the elected members of the Irish House of Commons were controlled by British government patronage. Westminster also retained control of the appointment of the Irish executive, including the lord lieutenant, which meant that British ministers continued to be the de facto governors of Ireland. Support for reform among Irish MPs was far from unanimous, however. In a parliament entirely composed of a wealthy, conservative Protestant élite, few were willing to contemplate changes which would endanger their powerful position, especially if this involved extending voting rights to the disenfranchised mass, comprising three million Catholics, Presbyterians and the Church of Ireland poor.

Then, in 1789, the outbreak of revolution in France delivered a dramatic stimulus to this moribund Irish polity. Stirring, momentous ideas circulated: the 'rights of man' to 'liberty, property, security and resistance to oppression'; the notion that 'sovereignty resides in the nation' rather than the king; the view that a people has the moral right to decide its own destiny. Inspired by these revolutionary ideals and eager to adapt them to Irish conditions, a group of educated, mostly middle-class Church of Ireland and Presbyterian radicals formed the Society of United Irishmen in Belfast, a city which was a hotbed of radical thought, and also in Dublin, in 1791. A young Dublin Protestant lawyer, Theobald Wolfe Tone (1763–98), emerged as the leader of this radical organisation, which aimed to unite Irishmen of all religions behind a programme of parliamentary reform, including the enfranchisement of Catholics, and so end Britain's domination of Irish affairs. After 1795 the movement assumed an overtly republican and separatist character. Tone himself outlined his political motives in his autobiography with succinct eloquence:

> To subvert the tyranny of our execrable Government, to break the connection with England, the never-failing source of all our political evils, and to assert the independence of my country – these were my objects. To unite the whole people of Ireland, to abolish the memory of all past dissensions, and to substitute the common name of Irishman in place of the denominations of Protestant, Catholic and Dissenter – these were my means.

His espousal of such radical separatist ideals led to Tone becoming the acknowledged founder of Irish republican nationalism, and his grave at Bodenstown in County Kildare is still the site of an annual pilgrimage by Irish nationalists of all shades of opinion.

The renewed outbreak of war between Britain and France in early 1793 prompted the authorities to take action to curb the spread of revolutionary republicanism in Ireland and so prevent the French from capitalising on Irish disaffection. Irish Catholic discontent was appeased by the passing of two Relief Acts which enfranchised Catholic smallholders and removed more of the existing penal laws, though the prohibition on Catholics entering parliament remained. In 1795 the Irish parliament, prompted by the British government, was even prepared to support the establishment of a national Catholic seminary at Maynooth in County Kildare, thus obviating the need for priests to go to the Continent to be educated, where they might be contaminated by republicanism. Fears that republican radicals might win over the Catholic peasantry led to the establishment of a government militia which many Catholics joined. On the other side, the United Irishmen saw themselves, and were seen by the authorities, as a much more revolutionary body than they had appeared at the start. In 1794 the organisation was declared illegal and driven underground.

Meanwhile, Tone had left Ireland for America, from where he eventually made his way to France. His persistent attempts to persuade the French government to sanction an expeditionary Irish force eventually bore fruit in December 1796, when a large fleet of forty-four ships carrying an army of fourteen thousand men set sail under General Lazare Hoche. However, when they arrived at Bantry Bay in County Cork they were prevented from landing by a strong headwind which turned into a gale. After a frustrating ten-day wait, they were forced to abort the attempted invasion and returned to France. As in 1688, a 'Protestant wind' exerted a decisive effect upon the course of history, causing some devout Protestants to discern a mark of divine intervention. It is indeed arguable that the elements saved Britain from military defeat at the hands of one of the largest invasion forces ever to threaten the British Isles.

The government's relief was only temporary, however. Since their suppression in 1794, the United Irishmen had reorganised themselves as a secret oath-bound society intent upon building up a nationwide military network in preparation for an insurrection. In addition to canvassing French support, they sought to mobilise the formidable but fragmented forces of the mainly rural Catholic Defenders behind their revolutionary agenda. One common means of mustering Defender support was to appeal to crude sectarian prejudices by invoking the spectre of Orange terror, since many Orangemen were now taking the government side and joining the ranks of the newly formed, overwhelmingly Protestant, yeomanry. Thus, ancient sectarian prejudices among the peasantry were beginning to dilute the original egalitarian aspirations of the intellectual middle class. The radical republican theory of a national rebellion transcending cleavages of class and creed was beginning to unravel in the face of intractable Irish realities.

In the immediate aftermath of the failed invasion at Bantry Bay, the British authorities stepped up their attempts to suppress the United Irishmen. In 1797 General Gerard Lake, commander of the crown forces in Ireland, conducted a campaign of military repression against republican radicals in Ulster, using a regular army augmented by a forty-thousand-strong yeomanry force and twenty thousand militia. The United Irishmen's organisational coherence and rebellious resolve were seriously undermined by a series of arrests, the seizure of large quantities of arms and the killing or transportation of those found guilty of administering or taking an illegal oath. The indiscriminate brutality of the troops drove many out of the organisation, while creating a lasting hatred in the hearts and minds of others. Lake's terror tactics were backed up by the government's effective spy and informer network, which meant that the identity of most of the leaders of the United Irishmen was known to the authorities in Dublin Castle by the time they had finalised their plans for rebellion in 1798. These plans were dealt a severe blow in March of that year, when fourteen of the principal conspirators were seized in Dublin. Lord Edward Fitzgerald (1763–98), one of the chief rebel organisers, escaped, but was later apprehended and fatally wounded. The part played by Fitzgerald in these events is remarkable. Unlike Tone and most of the northern rebel leaders, he was a Protestant aristocrat who had distinguished himself as a soldier and Irish parliamentarian before becoming attracted to revolutionary thought in the early 1790s.

Despite this setback, sufficient leaders and organisation remained and in late May an uprising began in several parts of Leinster with its epicentre at Wexford. The Wexford rising of mainly Catholic peasants with local middle-class leadership was initially successful. For a short while a republic was established in Wexford town, where the people addressed each other as 'Citizen' and changed the calendar to the 'Year One' after the manner of the French. On 21 June, however, the insurgents were crushed by superior government forces at the Battle of Vinegar Hill. Recent historical scholarship has refuted much of the conventional interpretation of the Wexford revolt as one of ignorant, disorganised peasants, goaded into rebellion by sectarian hatred. Certainly opportunities were taken to settle old scores and Protestants were gruesomely massacred at Scullabogue and on Wexford Bridge after the discipline of the United Irishmen had broken down. Rumours of sectarian atrocities quickly spread to Ulster where they played a large part in alienating Protestants from the United Irish insurrection. After the rebellion ended, the authorities highlighted this aspect and played down the republican and democratic elements, thereby helping to endorse a sectarian interpretation of the rising. In early June in the north-eastern counties of Antrim and Down an uneasy coalition of Presbyterians and Catholics tried to assert the 'rights of man' and bring about an Irish republic through force. Within a week, however, Henry Joy McCracken's band of rebels had been defeated at Antrim and a similar fate befell those led by Henry Munro at Ballynahinch in County Down. In the north as in the south, the government militia carried out savage reprisals in the wake of the rebels' defeat.

The final episode of the 1798 rebellion took place in County Mayo. In August a long-awaited contingent of French soldiers, a little over a thousand strong, under General Jean Humbert, arrived at Killala Bay to raise a revolt in the west. Three or four months earlier, French intervention might have proved decisive; now it was too late. Mayo was one of the poorest Irish counties and Connacht was the province where the United Irishmen had made least headway. The French were joined by a number of poorer Gaelic-speaking peasants who helped Humbert's army to rout Lake's forces at Castlebar and set up a republic of Connacht. Substantial rebel support proved unforthcoming, however, and the French surrendered to the combined forces of Generals Lake and Cornwallis at Ballinamuck, County Longford, on 8 September. By the time a second fleet arrived in October, carrying Theobald Wolfe Tone and three thousand French troops, the initiative was firmly with the government militia, who captured them at Lough Swilly in County Donegal. Anticipating execution, Tone, a figure much influenced by the ideals of the eighteenth-century Enlightenment, asked that he be shot as a soldier rather than hanged as a common criminal, in keeping with his rank of general in the French army. The refusal of his request led him to take his own life in prison in November 1798.

The 1798 rising failed for a number of reasons. Rebel organisation and co-ordination were poor, government military strength was vastly superior and French aid was inadequate and ill-timed. At an ideological level, the secular, non-sectarian republican ideals of Tone and the United Irishmen were not borne out in practice. Though the rebellion witnessed the involvement of Catholic peasants, Presbyterian merchants and a Protestant aristocrat, their motives and objectives were disparate and contradictory, ranging from separatist nationalism to social grievance. Indeed, it could be said that a movement which set out to ameliorate the existing divisions in Irish society ended up exacerbating them. Undoubtedly, the whole process of mass politicisation is a key element in helping to explain the causes of the rising. Like many revolutions, it was marked by savage brutality on both sides, often going far beyond the military interests of the contestants. The defeated troops of Humbert were afforded full military honours and permitted to return to France, while the Irish rebels were punished ruthlessly.

Inevitably the rebellion left its legends and its martyrs, none more revered than Tone. Nationalists would remember the rising for the merciless behaviour of government troops; opponents of the rising for the anti-Protestant atrocities of Wexford. It remains one of the bloodiest episodes in modern Irish history, with an estimated thirty thousand deaths in total, many more than died during the Terror in France. The ideological legacy of 1798 was certainly profound. It established the concept of a republic as the holy grail of Irish nationalists, a political aspiration pure enough to die for. Yet because the original republican ideal was heterogeneous, even contradictory, in nature, Irish republicanism, in the words of historian K. Theodore Hoppen, 'became an extremely eclectic phenomenon from which almost all groups could pick what they wanted and reject what they disliked'. The ambiguous legacy of what has been called 'the Tone cult' is still in evidence today, as constitutional Irish nationalists honour Tone's non-sectarian radicalism, while militant republicans invoke his revolutionary separatism.

The most important immediate consequence of the 1798 rebellion was the passing of the Act of Union between Great Britain and Ireland in 1800. The arguments in favour of legislative union – which, after all, had worked in the case of England and Scotland in 1707 – were compelling from a British government perspective. The Irish parliament had been ineffective during the course of the rising. With the war against France still going on, the strategic defence interests of Britain could not afford to allow a semi-independent, rebellious Ireland to continue to pose a threat to its security. Not only was direct control from Westminster considered the most effective means of keeping Ireland quiescent, but the prime minister, William Pitt (1759–1806), believed that the abolition of the ineffectual and sometimes obstinate Irish parliament would remove a major source of Catholic disaffection, especially if coupled with a measure of emancipation for Catholics in a new constitutional arrangement.

The idea of union was far from universally popular on either side of the Irish Sea. Many people in Britain had the deepest distaste for Pitt and all his works and in this particular case considered he was encumbering them with a potentially dangerous liability. Many Irish parliamentarians, Protestant to a man, were initially outraged by this gross infringement of their constitutional independence, but gradually realised that in the new structure they would be part of a large Protestant majority in the United Kingdom rather than a minority in Ireland. Orangemen opposed Pitt's proposals because they saw in them the seeds of Catholic hegemony in Ireland. Many Irish Catholics, on the other hand, were encouraged to support the proposed Union because it promised emancipation, though the issue was of little relevance to the peasant majority for whom parliamentary representation was a distant dream.

The government's first Union Bill was narrowly defeated in the Irish parliament in 1799. Pitt pressed ahead, however, making full use of his most effective weapon, the power of the purse. Though his methods would be scandalous in the modern era, government patronage was an accepted part of eighteenth-century political culture. Sinecures, pensions and direct money payments were commonly used to ensure electoral support and reward parliamentary allies. That said, the scale of government-sponsored bribery and fraud employed to persuade the Irish parliament to vote itself out of existence in February 1800 was unprecedented. It is ironical that Pitt, who used this power of bribery to such tremendous effect upon others, was personally incorruptible and eventually died with large debts.

The resultant Act of Union decreed that Ireland would henceforth send one hundred MPs to the British House of Commons and thirty-two peers (including four bishops) to the House of Lords. The established Churches of England and Ireland were recognised, and a free trade area between the two countries was created. But though the parliament at College Green was abolished, the executive at Dublin Castle was retained. Social legislation and taxation were often very different in the two countries, indicating that Ireland's integration was destined to be less than complete and its distinctiveness was to prove a source of continual political tension. Britain's attitude to Ireland was to be confused and ambiguous throughout the nineteenth century; at times it was viewed as an integral part of the United Kingdom, at other times as a half-alien dependency.

Where Pitt failed disastrously was in his aim to reconcile the large Catholic majority in Ireland to the Union by Catholic emancipation, which would have removed the disabilities under which they laboured and would have given them, among other things, the right to sit in the United Kingdom parliament. Pitt was a man of large vision and he realised that the success of the Union would ultimately depend on the willingness of people on both sides of the Irish Sea to accept it as a sensible and equitable arrangement. The rock on which emancipation foundered was King George III. Integrity and obstinacy were two of the most marked features in his character and both were brought into full play when he decided that assenting to emancipation would violate his coronation oath. He was prepared to abdicate, but not to sign. Yet the king was by no means the only objector to Catholic emancipation. Virulent anti-Catholicism was never far from the surface in eighteenth-century British sentiment, and one may reasonably doubt whether emancipation could have been carried through parliament, even if the king had not stood in Pitt's way. In the end, however, it was Pitt who went. A few weeks after the Union was set up, the prime minister surrendered his seals of office and the king selected the utterly undistinguished Henry Addington, later Viscount Sidmouth, to take his place. Pitt returned to office in 1804 but by that time Catholic emancipation was no longer a political possibility.

Though its short-term impact was slight, the Act of Union fundamentally altered the relationship between Britain and Ireland in the longer term. It was no love match, but a shotgun marriage, sadly lacking in connubial bliss, designed to control Ireland. Whereas the Union and its undoing became the singular obsession of nationalist Ireland over the next 120 years, the settlement of 1800 held no such significance for Britain, Ireland being but one of London's many imperial preoccupations. Within Ireland itself, the Union polarised political opinion and strengthened the religious divide in ways few could have foreseen in 1800. Pitt's failure to deliver on his promise of emancipation engendered feelings of betrayal among many Catholics and predisposed them to support campaigns for repeal and independence, thereby leading to the exclusive identification of the Irish nation with the Catholic nation. Church of Ireland Protestants and Presbyterians, conversely, came to develop strong pro-Union sympathies, especially in the north-east, the region which prospered most under the Union.

Thus, the settlement which was intended to unite hearts and minds proved to be deeply divisive for Irish and Anglo-Irish political relations. Moreover, the economies of the two countries were widely divergent, a predominantly agricultural Ireland having little in common with a rapidly industrialising Britain. Consequently, few Irish industries could compete effectively with those of their neighbour and the country was not seen as an attractive site for British investment. Such socio-economic problems were compounded by the manifest religious, cultural and linguistic differences between the two countries, all of which served to highlight Ireland's separateness from the rest of the United Kingdom. As democratic procedures developed gradually within Britain and Ireland, and numbers became more important than property ownership in electoral politics, it was inevitable that the voice of the Catholic majority would demand to be heard. As ultimate responsibility for Irish affairs now lay at Westminster, this ever more insistent voice became an increasingly disruptive part of the British body politic.

3

EMANCIPATION AND REPEAL
1801–1848

Among the arguments advanced by William Pitt in favour of the Act of Union was his contention that this was the constitutional arrangement 'most likely to give Ireland security, quiet, and internal repose'. The vanity of his hopes was to be repeatedly exposed as the nineteenth century unfolded, beginning with the ineffectual rising of Robert Emmet (1778–1803) in 1803. Emmet, a middle-class Dublin Protestant, was a member of the fragmented United Irish network which survived the purges of 1798. Encouraged by the renewal of the Anglo-French war in May 1803 and hoping for a Napoleonic invasion of England, he led an attack on Dublin Castle on 23 July which was intended to act as a catalyst for a spontaneous nationwide insurrection to establish 'a free and independent republic'. The rising was quickly aborted, however, largely because of Emmet's inept organisational and leadership skills. He was captured, convicted of treason and publicly hanged in Thomas Street in Dublin in September. Though Emmet's rebellious gesture changed nothing at the time, later revolutionaries such as Patrick Pearse would cherish 'the memory of a sacrifice Christ-like in its perfection' and draw inspiration from the mythic power of his speech from the dock, in which he declared: 'Let no man write my epitaph... When my country takes her place among the nations of the earth, then, and not till then, let my epitaph be written.'

If Emmet's rising proved anything, it was that radical republicanism had lost its popular appeal in early-nineteenth-century Ireland. Political discourse was becoming focused instead on an altogether different constitutional issue, that of Catholic emancipation. Although Irish Catholics had been granted the right to vote on the same terms as Protestants in the 1790s, they remained excluded from parliament and from state and municipal office. When Prime Minister Pitt's support for the inclusion of some measure of Catholic emancipation in the Act of Union foundered on parliamentary and royal opposition, Irish Catholic disaffection was left to simmer into the 1800s. Initially, the issue of emancipation was primarily of concern to a minority of Catholics, mainly those ambitious members of the middle class whose professional advancement was impeded by discriminatory laws. Such restrictions were largely irrelevant to the impoverished peasant majority, desperately trying to eke out a livelihood on sub-divided plots of land. By the 1820s, however, a leader had emerged who was capable of uniting these disparate Catholic classes behind a revitalised crusade for emancipation, thereby transforming the character of the campaign from a polite sectional pressure group into a vigorous mass movement. This leader was Daniel O'Connell (1775–1847).

Born into a Catholic landowning family in County Kerry, O'Connell established a national reputation as a lawyer before turning his attention to the emancipation issue in the early 1800s. Staunchly royalist and socially conservative, he abhorred the revolutionary separatism of the United Irishmen, while sympathising with their desire for parliamentary reform. It was O'Connell's passionate belief that Irish Catholics would be loyal subjects of the king if they were granted equality of status with their Protestant compatriots. In 1823 he established the Catholic Association to agitate for emancipation, using all available constitutional means. The most striking feature of the association was the admission of the Catholic poor as associate members for a subscription of one penny per month, a fee known as the 'Catholic rent', which was used to provide legal assistance and compensation for victimised freeholders. This innovation led to the unprecedented mass mobilisation of the Irish peasantry as a coherent, disciplined, non-violent political force. For the first time in modern Irish history the democratic potential of Catholic Ireland was harnessed in the pursuit of fundamental political change. The association also secured the active support of the influential Catholic clergy, thereby forging a new and powerful alliance between Catholicism and nationalism, which proved to be of enduring importance in Ireland's subsequent historical development. The Catholic Association represents an important landmark in British as well as Irish politics, for it was the first example of a cohesive, non-revolutionary movement based on mass support.

By the mid-1820s the campaign for Catholic emancipation had acquired an irresistible national momentum under O'Connell's radical, charismatic leadership. The first demonstration of the electoral power of this dynamic new movement came in the general election of 1826, when large numbers of tenant farmers defied their landlords by voting for liberal, pro-emancipation Protestant candidates. The obstinacy of this hitherto biddable electorate sent a tremor through the ranks of the Protestant oligarchy in Ireland and worried the British government. Two years later, O'Connell himself took the remarkable step of standing for election against a government candidate in a County Clare by-election. As a Catholic, he was not entitled to sit in parliament, but there was no law which prevented him from standing as a candidate. His resounding victory raised the immediate prospect of the election of many more Irish Catholic MPs, disabled from sitting in parliament. At best, this would turn the Union parliament into a farce; at worst, it could lead to violence on an uncontrollable scale.

O'Connell's by-election victory marks the birth of Irish democracy, therefore, for it was this event that finally forced the government's hand. Alarmed by the unprecedented expression of popular feeling and fearing its translation into violent rebellion – a fear shrewdly exploited by O'Connell – the prime minister, the Duke of Wellington, supported by Sir Robert Peel, decided to submit to the democratic will. In April 1829 the Catholic Emancipation Act was passed into law, thus clearing the way for Catholics to enter parliament and hold high civil and military office. O'Connell was not allowed to take his seat immediately, but was duly admitted after a new by-election contest. Though the tangible benefits of the Act were confined to a small minority of Irish Catholics, its symbolic significance had a much wider resonance. It represented a striking psychological role reversal for those who seemed forever destined to play the part of the vanquished in Ireland's historical drama and bequeathed an instructive moral to later nationalists. As Gearóid Ó Tuathaigh has written: 'The Government had yielded through fear what it had refused to the force of rational argument or basic justice. The lesson was obvious – Britain would not concede anything to Ireland except under the threat of revolution.' The Catholic masses were beginning to come into their own.

Following this historic victory, Ireland's 'Liberator', as O'Connell came to be affectionately known, turned his attention to his second great political objective and the one that dominated his parliamentary career: the repeal of the Union and the restoration of the Irish parliament. In 1830 he formed the Society for the Repeal of the Union and set about seeking parliamentary support for the creation of an independent Irish legislature under the British crown. It should be stressed that O'Connell was no separatist; on the contrary, he argued that repealing the Union would strengthen the people's loyalty to the British monarch by removing a festering grievance. But whereas emancipation could be conceded, albeit reluctantly, by Westminster, the repeal of the Union was non-negotiable because it would threaten the fundamental unity of the United Kingdom.

The futility of O'Connell's campaign was confirmed in 1834 when his pro-repeal motion was heavily defeated in the House of Commons. Chastened by this experience, he turned instead to the pursuit of Irish reforms under the existing Union framework. He entered into a parliamentary alliance with the ruling Whig Party, the so-called Lichfield House compact, whereby O'Connellite MPs agreed to support the Whigs in return for reforms of the tithe system and municipal government. His abandonment of the repeal issue was merely temporary, however, and in July 1840 he renewed his agitation with the foundation of the Loyal National Repeal Association.

After a sluggish start, the campaign gathered momentum in 1842, aided by a group of new allies known as the Young Irelanders. These were a band of idealistic middle-class intellectuals led by Thomas Davis (1814–45), a Protestant barrister from Cork, who in 1842 co-founded the *Nation* newspaper with Charles Gavan Duffy (1816–1903), a northern Catholic, to spread the gospel of repeal and promote their pluralist, non-sectarian, nationalist views. This movement had strong parallels with other European groups such as Giuseppe Mazzini's Young Italy. The trusted tactics of the emancipation campaign were revived. A 'repeal rent', modelled on the Catholic rent of the 1820s, was collected, and the support and participation of the Catholic priesthood again enlisted. The year 1843 witnessed the emergence of 'monster meetings', a powerfully effective new tactic. These were vast, open-air political rallies, often held at places of historic significance, at which O'Connell would stir his massive audiences to euphoric heights with his militant rhetoric, while simultaneously stressing his allegiance to the British crown and constitution.

Despite O'Connell's sincere disavowal of violence as a means to political ends, the government saw the alarming spectre of mass revolt behind such demonstrations of moral force and decided to exorcise it. The moment of confrontation came in October 1843 when Prime Minister Peel banned a monster meeting scheduled for Clontarf near Dublin. Reluctant to risk violence and bloodshed, O'Connell cancelled the rally, though this did not prevent his subsequent arrest and imprisonment on a spurious conspiracy charge. His conviction, which was later quashed on appeal, came as a devastating blow to a man whose whole political career was based upon a fastidious respect for the law of the land. If the momentum of the repeal movement seemed irresistible before this confrontation, it lost its essential impetus after Clontarf and led some of his supporters to question the capacity of O'Connell's constitutional methods to bring about change on this key issue. O'Connell had certainly miscalculated and his commanding leadership of Catholic Ireland had been fatally undermined.

Having failed in his bid to bring extra-parliamentary pressure to bear on the government, O'Connell gravitated towards more conventional parliamentary tactics to achieve his goal of repeal. As in the 1830s, he sought to further his cause by forging an alliance with the Whig Party which again came to power in June 1846. This strategy, however, alienated many idealistic Young Irelanders, who accused O'Connell of compromise. He, in turn, resented their purist aloofness and resolved to reassert his authority over them. At a meeting of the Repeal Association in July 1846 he demanded from all members an absolute renunciation of violence as a political weapon.

Though still committed to non-violent methods in practice, the Young Irelanders refused to rule out the use of physical force in theory. One radical voice, that of Thomas Francis Meagher (1822–67), even went so far as to eulogise the sword as 'a sacred weapon'. Such language was anathema to O'Connellites and their protests led to the secession of the Young Irelanders from the association. The bond between Young and 'Old' Ireland was finally, and irrevocably, broken. In 1847 O'Connell died. No other Irish politician would be able to aspire to a fraction of his authority for many years to come.

In early 1847 the disaffected Young Irelanders formed a new association, the Irish Confederation, under William Smith O'Brien (1803–64), a Protestant landlord and MP. The confederation differed little in aims or objectives from the Repeal Association, being committed to the restoration of Irish self-government by non-violent means. Its united front was short-lived, however. With the country ravaged by chronic starvation, a rift developed between pro-landlord moderates like Smith O'Brien and more radical thinkers like James Fintan Lalor (1807–49), who espoused a revolutionary theory of land reform based on peasant proprietorship, claiming that 'the entire ownership of Ireland, moral and material, is vested of right in the people of Ireland'.

Lalor's social radicalism attracted the support of a minority of confederation members, notably John Mitchel (1815–75), who left the organisation in February 1848 and founded the *United Irishman* newspaper, through which he sought to inspire a revolutionary nationalist fervour. His efforts were greatly enhanced by the popular rising which swept the monarchy from power in France in February 1848 and radiated a mood of revolutionary excitement across Europe. Hitherto cautious confederation members were imbued with a new spirit of defiance and Mitchel himself openly called for the establishment of an Irish republic by force of arms.

Alarmed by this revolutionary ferment, the British government arrested Mitchel, Smith O'Brien and Meagher on sedition charges in March. In May, Mitchel was sentenced to fourteen years' transportation to Australia. Two months later, after further arrests, the government declared membership of the confederation illegal, thus provoking the rebel leadership to attempt a desperate act of insurrection. Without any proper military or tactical planning, Smith O'Brien tried to rouse a starving and dispirited Munster peasantry into rebellion in the closing days of July. His efforts proved pathetically fruitless and culminated in a farcical skirmish with police at Ballingarry, County Tipperary. Smith O'Brien himself referred to the incident as an 'escapade', though the event subsequently acquired the more disparaging epithet of 'the battle of the Widow McCormick's cabbage patch', recalling the owner of the garden where the fiasco occurred. At the time, the 1848 'rising' merely marked the humiliating demise of the Young Irelanders. Later, however, it assumed a somewhat mythic significance in the historical continuum of revolutionary nationalism stretching back to Emmet and Tone, not least because among those wounded at Ballingarry was a young man named James Stephens (1825–1901), who would shortly resuscitate the corpse of revolutionary nationalism by helping to found a far more enduring militant movement, Fenianism.

4

THE GREAT FAMINE
1845–1851

The Great Famine of the 1840s was the greatest human catastrophe in Irish history. Chief among the many factors which caused it was the system of land tenure in nineteenth-century Ireland. This whole system required radical restructuring, but no British government of the time could have taken on the landlords and interfered with the sacred rights of private property, even if it had wished to do so. During the early part of the century competition for land became intense among a rapidly expanding population, which had grown to over eight million by 1841. This land hunger encouraged the practice of multiple subdivision, whereby small holdings were parcelled into increasingly smaller plots which were sub-let in turn to the poorest families. The result was a social pyramid of (often absentee) landlord, tenant farmer, cottier and landless agricultural labourer.

Those at the base of this inherently unbalanced structure

maintained a precarious level of subsistence. Rents were high, few owned the land they worked and security of tenure was rare, except in parts of the north where a system known as the 'Ulster custom' prevailed, which entitled an evicted tenant to compensation for improvements carried out during his tenancy. Many tenants were cottiers, that is, peasants occupying a very small portion of land which was let annually to the highest bidder. British observers often made the mistake of assuming that because Irish and English land law were virtually identical, social relationships were also equivalent. In fact, they were radically different. English landowners usually lived on their estates and shared the religion of their tenants, to whom they would often extend charity and a benign paternalism. English landlords in Ireland, however, were mostly alien in religion and sometimes in language from their tenants, whom they commonly saw in the narrowest economic terms. Indeed all too often they were absentees, glad to leave the administration of their estates to agents whose principal remit was to secure the maximum possible revenue.

The situation in Ireland was made worse by the fact that by the 1840s some three million peasants were dependent upon a single crop for sustenance: the potato. Cheap, convenient and nutritious, a sufficient quantity of potatoes could be grown on an acre of ground to feed a family of five for six months. The health of the vegetable could not be relied upon, however, and many people died as a result of potato shortages in the period prior to 1845. Indeed, the massive scale and devastating impact of the Great Famine has tended to overshadow the fact that intermittent crop failures and food shortages were an integral part of Irish and European life in the preceding centuries. In 1739–41 Ireland was racked by a famine of such severity that some historians have estimated that more lives were lost in relative terms in these two years than during the 1840s. Less acute subsistence crises occurred in 1816–19, 1821–22 and 1830–31. Deaths from starvation and attendant disease resulted during each of these periods, though mortality rates were kept at a relatively low level as a result of a combination of government aid and private charity.

What was unprecedented about the 1840s, however, was the prolonged nature of the crop failure and the persistence of the new potato blight, *Phytophthora infestans*. Initially, it was hoped that the outbreak of the disease in the autumn of 1845 would prove to be an ecological aberration, but such hopes had evaporated within the year, as the 1846 crop failed completely. There was a partial failure in 1847, followed by another total collapse in 1848. The blight continued until 1851, leaving behind a dreadful legacy of human misery, social devastation and political recrimination. Precise figures are difficult to calculate, but most historians accept that around one million people died of starvation and the diseases which accompanied it, while more than another million emigrated between 1846 and 1852. Inevitably, mortality rates were highest among the poorest inhabitants of the poorest regions. Large areas of Connacht and Munster suffered the greatest population loss, and though the north and east escaped the worst ravages of the disaster, thousands perished in the fetid slums of Dublin and Belfast, which were swollen by hordes of rural destitutes.

A measure of the depopulation from famine, disease and emigration can be seen by comparing the census returns of 1841 and 1851. In 1841 the population of Ireland was well over eight million; in 1851 it had dropped to six and a half million, a decline of almost 20 per cent. The decline was over 25 per cent in every county in the province of Connacht and even exceeded 30 per cent in County Roscommon. At a time when the population of nearly every county in England, Scotland and Wales was rising, only two Irish counties – Antrim and

Dublin – showed a decline of less than 10 per cent.

Initial responsibility for dealing with the 1845 crisis fell to Conservative Prime Minister Sir Robert Peel (1788–1850). He reacted swiftly to alleviate suffering by issuing grants to local relief committees, instituting public relief works, setting up food depots to store and distribute imported Indian meal and repealing the Corn Laws in 1846. The latter measure, which was prompted partly by fears that famine would affect the British working classes, led to the collapse of the Peel administration and a damaging split in the Tory Party. In the summer of 1846 a new Whig government came to power under the leadership of Lord John Russell (1792–1878) and initiated a significant shift in famine relief policy which proved to be tragic for Ireland.

The key figures in providing relief were Charles Wood, the new chancellor of the Exchequer, and Charles Trevelyan, permanent secretary at the Treasury. Both were firm believers in the economic doctrine of *laissez faire* which dictated that the state should not normally interfere in trade or private enterprise, but allow market forces to operate freely. In a pre-welfare-state era it was considered the proper role of government to promote self-sufficiency and discourage state dependency. Thus, the concept of minimum state intervention became the guiding principle of Russell's Irish famine policy. Food depots were closed and the provision of food to the destitute was entrusted to private enterprise. The state did establish a public works scheme, but this was to be paid for by Irish taxpayers, especially the negligent landlords, in the belief that 'Irish property should pay for Irish poverty'. Similarly, much of the £7 million total spent on famine relief by the government was advanced in the form of loans, repayable with interest from the local rates. What the Russell administration failed to appreciate, however, was that Ireland simply did not have the financial resources to deal with a calamity of such horrific proportions. In particular, Trevelyan's argument for the transfer of responsibility for relief to the Irish Poor Law in 1847 ignored the complete inadequacy of this system in Ireland. Irish poverty had few European parallels, certainly to the west of the Russian empire.

As the crisis worsened, increasing numbers of starving families became dependent upon the relief works. By the spring of 1847 almost three-quarters of a million people, approximately one in three adult males, were employed in such tasks as road-building and hill-levelling. The physically demanding nature of the work meant that the weakest and most needy could not participate directly and so were unable to benefit. They, like many others, were often left to suffer a slow, wretched death.

Government concern about the accumulating cost of the public works schemes resulted in Trevelyan ordering their closure in the summer of 1846, but a public outcry led to them continuing until 1847, when they were replaced by a direct relief programme. Temporary soup kitchens were then set up to distribute free food to the hungry, the number of which stood at an appalling three million by this time. In September the soup kitchen scheme was replaced by an outdoor relief system which meant that the poor could receive cooked food without having to be admitted to the already desperately overcrowded workhouses. The receipt of relief was dependent on the fulfilment of certain preconditions, however. These included a labour test, whereby the poor were required to break stones for up to ten hours a day before they were fed, and the 'quarter-acre clause', which rendered tenants who occupied more than a quarter-acre of land ineligible for free rations. Despite these deterrents, the outdoor relief scheme had become the main source of food for an incredible 800,000 people by

June 1848, with as many again clamouring for rations within the workhouse walls.

The winter of 1846–47, the severest in living memory, heaped misery upon misery. Contagious diseases had reached epidemic proportions and though several hundred temporary fever hospitals were opened, thousands succumbed to typhus, cholera, relapsing fever and scurvy. Mass burials were common, frequently by means of the reusable trap coffin. Tragically, many doctors, priests and relief workers died from fever as a direct result of their selfless efforts to ease the suffering of the sick and dying. Children were among the most numerous and pathetic famine victims. Thousands were orphaned, abandoned in workhouses or simply deserted by desperate parents, who preferred to take their chances on the emigrant ship rather than await certain death at home. Several charitable and religious groups generously devoted their limited resources to voluntary famine relief, especially the Quakers, who made prodigious efforts to counteract mass starvation by distributing free rice and establishing soup kitchens in many areas of the country. Others behaved less honourably, notably a minority of proselytising Church of Ireland zealots who, in exchange for free food, sought to win converts to Protestantism from among the starving Catholic peasantry, a practice which earned the emotive epithet 'souperism'.

In the summer of 1847 Russell's government declared the Famine officially over, though hundreds continued to perish daily. The purpose of this declaration was to transfer the responsibility for relief to the Irish taxpayer. The government's insistence on the collection of rates greatly increased the financial burden on Irish landlords and caused many to fall into debt as the crisis escalated. This had serious consequences for their tenants, as indebted landlords started to evict destitute tenants who were unable to pay rent, let alone rates, to make way for wealthier ones. This led to the mass clearances of smallholders, especially in the west of Ireland, which witnessed many harrowing scenes of sick and dying families being forcibly evicted.

The Encumbered Estates (Ireland) Act of 1849, under which bankrupt landlords could sell their debt-ridden estates, served merely to make matters worse. A similar measure had recently been passed for England, with apparently beneficial results for landlords and tenants alike. In Ireland the effect was very different. The Act, which led to the sale of three thousand estates over the next decade, the majority to middle-class Catholic entrepreneurs, proved to be a bitter pill for the Irish peasantry, thousands of whom were evicted by the new estate owners to make way for grazing and the consolidation of holdings. This piece of legislation, which was intended to expedite the socio-economic transformation of Ireland desired by many British ministers and officials, represents a striking example of the very common misconception that methods which had worked in England would also work in Ireland.

For the dispossessed multitudes, emigration became the only alternative to death. One-quarter of a million people left Ireland in 1847, with another million following over the next five years, mainly to Britain, North America and Australia. Thousands of transatlantic famine refugees died in transit amidst the appalling squalor of the notorious coffin ships. Of those who survived, few were ever to return, though many harboured a deep-seated anglophobic resentment and a determination to play a role in ending British rule in Ireland. Residual traces of such anglophobia are still visible among latter-day Irish-American republicans, many of whom take their political bearings from folk memories of famine-induced suffering at the hands of the British.

The Famine had a profound impact upon Ireland's

demographic, social and economic structures. It established a pattern of population decline, underpinned by high emigration and low marriage and birth rates, which became unique in Europe and was not finally reversed until the 1960s. In post-Famine Ireland emigration became an accepted, even expected, fact of life for generations of Irish men and women. It also led to the virtual disappearance of the cottier class and the elimination of very small holdings. Farms were no longer divided at inheritance between sons, but usually went to the eldest male, a practice which encouraged delayed marriages, low birth rates and further emigration. This led in turn to a deterioration of the position of women in society. Faced with the prospect of a narrowly restricted life in rural Ireland, many young single women opted to leave, making this type of emigration a unique feature of the Irish experience.

The Famine also delivered a major blow to the already weakening position of the Irish language and compounded the association of Gaelic with poverty, ignorance and failure. Many of those who died or emigrated were Irish-speaking peasants, with the result that by 1851 the number of Gaelic speakers had fallen to fewer than two million. But famine was not the only factor which hastened the decline of Irish as the first language of the Catholic masses in nineteenth-century Ireland. The introduction of a national system of elementary education in 1831 represented a decisive turning-point in the fortunes of the language. The national schools, as they were known, provided free, state-sponsored education through the sole medium of English, thereby confirming its superior utility as the language of international commerce and culture. In a country where emigration was an inescapable social fact for most poor communities, many Irish-speaking parents co-operated with the schools in encouraging their children to abandon Irish in favour of English, in order to enhance their prospects of success elsewhere. Such socio-economic pragmatism was endorsed by no less a figure than Daniel O'Connell who, though a fluent Gaelic speaker himself, addressed his mass political audiences in English and once remarked that he could witness the death of the Irish language without so much as a sigh.

But while the Famine has undoubtedly left deep scars upon the Irish psyche and society, its legacy has not been entirely debilitating. The remarkably generous response of the Irish public to recent famines in the developing world is perhaps one indication of how the national memory of past sufferings has inspired a genuine concern for the present privations of Africa and Asia. This is certainly a view endorsed by former President Mary Robinson, who has suggested that Ireland's past gives its people 'a moral viewpoint and an historically informed compassion on some of the events happening now'. Her own high-profile visits to famine-stricken African countries during her term of office epitomised this compassion, and in her role as United Nations Commissioner for Human Rights she remained committed to the relief of suffering in developing countries.

For many in Ireland, the British government's response to the Famine made a mockery of the Act of Union. They argued that Ireland had not been treated as an equal partner within the United Kingdom, but rather as a marginal inferior which was expected to cope alone with an appalling catastrophe. For them the Famine highlighted Ireland's essential separateness from Britain and exposed the underlying colonial nature of the relationship between the two countries. Unprecedented levels of human suffering had occurred at the centre of the richest empire in the world, yet through its doctrinaire policies the Whig government had allowed fiscal and ideological orthodoxies to take precedence over a more generous and humane response. The question posed by Dublin's *Freeman's Journal* cut to the heart of the matter: 'Is there justice or humanity in the world that such things could *be*, in the middle of the nineteenth century and within twelve hours' reach of the opulence, grandeur and power of a court and capital the first upon the earth?'

Others took a more malign view, seeing genocidal intent in Britain's famine policies. Such an interpretation was not confined to extreme nationalists like John Mitchel; even the lord lieutenant, Lord Clarendon, writing to Russell in 1849, urged him to desist from his 'policy of extermination'. Among the most enduring and bitter Irish Famine memories was that of cattle, grain and other foodstuffs being exported by Irish merchants while people starved. Most of these exports went to England to alleviate food shortages. Retrospective nationalist revulsion was also directed at the non-interventionism of Trevelyan, who was wont to regard the Famine as a punishment from God to teach the unreasonable Irish a lesson. Inspired by a mixture of *laissez-faire* doctrine and religious fatalism, he crudely recommended that the country be left to 'the operation of natural causes'.

Traditionally, most Irish historians steered clear of research and writing on the Famine. Over the last forty years the tendency of revisionist historians has been to play down the significance of the event and to minimise the inadequacy of the British government's response. More recently, post-revisionist historians have begun to highlight the suffering of the Irish people and criticise the failures and blind spots in British policy. Accusations of British culpability for the Famine have troubled the Anglo-Irish relationship even in the contemporary era. The continuing sensitivity of this issue was highlighted at a major Famine commemoration event held in Cork in the summer of 1997. The gathering prompted the new British prime minister, Tony Blair, to seek to heal this festering wound by formally acknowledging Britain's inadequate response to the Famine. In a remarkable message to the Irish people he stated:

> That one million people should have died in what was then part of the richest and most powerful nation in the world is something that still causes pain as we reflect on it today. Those who governed in London at the time failed their people through standing by while a crop failure turned into a massive human tragedy. We must not forget such a dreadful event.

While some were critical of the practice of a contemporary government effectively apologising for the deficiencies of its distant predecessor, the Irish government and most Irish people warmly welcomed Blair's comments, seeing them as a helpful contribution to Anglo-Irish understanding in the 1990s.

For a considerable time after the Famine, most Irish people were too traumatised to give much attention to either the political or social implications of the terrible experiences they had undergone. When it was possible to consider such matters, two different, but not inconsistent, conclusions came to be drawn in Ireland. One was that the land system required radical reform; the other, that no British government could properly appreciate Ireland's particular needs, and so could never govern the country to Ireland's benefit. These twin themes of land reform and self-government would dominate Irish political thought for the remainder of the century, and far into the next.

5
THE POLITICS OF NATIONALISM
1852–1878

The 1850s and 1860s were decades of slow recovery from the ravages of the Famine. Agricultural production and profits rose gradually during this period, bringing relative prosperity to many small farmers. The fundamental injustice of the land system remained, however, ensuring that agrarian reform would become one of the central issues of Irish politics in the late nineteenth century. Indeed, agitation for what were to become the key demands of Irish tenants – the 'three Fs', fair rent, fixity of tenure and free sale – was already being expressed in the early 1850s by the Irish Tenant League. Fair rent signified rent fixed by an independent body; fixity of tenure meant that a tenant who paid his rent and adhered to other tenurial covenants could not be evicted; free sale implied that when a tenant left his holding, the value of any improvements made should revert to him, not the landlord.

The league was founded in 1850 and consisted mostly of prosperous grain farmers who were primarily concerned with protecting their incomes during a short-term agricultural depression. Although it never managed to transcend its sectoral origins, it was instrumental in the creation of the independent Irish Party at Westminster, following the 1852 general election. League MPs formed an alliance with Irish members of a religious pressure group, the Catholic Defence Association, to extract agrarian and religious concessions from the British government through a policy of 'independent opposition'. The effectiveness of this alliance was soon destroyed, however, by sectarian divisions and the defection to government offices of two of its MPs. By the end of the decade this brief experiment in parliamentary agitation had withered away and in its place a reinvigorated revolutionary nationalist movement was taking shape.

On Saint Patrick's Day 1858 a secret revolutionary organisation, as yet unnamed, was established in Dublin and New York by veterans of the 1848 rising. James Stephens, fresh from a nationwide tour of the country to gauge the revolutionary mood, organised the movement in Ireland, while John O'Mahony and Michael Doheny were the American co-ordinators. It was O'Mahony who named the organisation the Fenian Brotherhood in honour of a warrior troop of ancient Irish legend, though the movement also became known as the Irish Republican Brotherhood (IRB). The Fenians' objective can be simply stated: the establishment of an independent, non-sectarian Irish republic by revolutionary means. As such, they invoked the historical memory of the 1798 rebellion and anticipated the rising of 1916. Within Ireland, they attracted support from among the working classes of town and country – shop assistants, small farmers, agricultural labourers – and also recruited to their ranks many disaffected Irish soldiers who had served in the British army. Abroad, they drew from the well of post-Famine anglophobia that flourished among immigrant Irish communities in America and Britain.

The Fenians made their first, striking impact on Irish political life in November 1861 when they organised the funeral of Terence Bellew McManus, another 1848 veteran, who died in poverty in San Francisco. McManus's remains were transported across America to New York, from where they were shipped to Cork and on to Dublin for burial. This marathon procession attracted large crowds at every stage and rekindled a nationalist fervour which had lain dormant for thirteen years. It also drew the wrath of the Irish Catholic Church in the formidable person of Archbishop, later Cardinal, Paul Cullen, who vehemently opposed Fenianism because it did not promote the Catholic interest. Yet even the vociferous opposition of the most influential Irish clergyman of the age did not prevent the movement gaining many clerical sympathisers.

By 1865, the promised 'year of action', Stephens estimated that the Fenian movement had grown to over eighty thousand members in Ireland, but they were crucially lacking in the arms and money vital to the success of an insurrection. Whereas earlier rebels had looked to France for military support, Stephens looked to America, his hopes boosted by news of the willingness of many of the several thousand Irishmen, who had enlisted on each side in the American Civil War, to fight for Ireland's freedom. Though some soldiers did travel to Ireland after the war ended, sufficient American support failed to materialise.

Stephens's revolutionary plans received a further setback when he and other Fenian leaders were arrested by the authorities in the autumn of 1865. His subsequent prison escape and flight to America resulted in little more than a revised, rhetorical resolution to strike in 1866. Eventually, in December of that year, the vacillating Stephens was deposed as head of the IRB and replaced by an Irish-American colonel, Thomas Kelly.

Kelly travelled to London in early 1867 to co-ordinate plans for a rising scheduled for 11 February. The military plan was for arms and ammunition to be seized from Chester Castle in England and shipped to Ireland for immediate use by Fenian units in the east and south-west. However, news that a government informer had infiltrated the movement led to the last-minute cancellation of the ambitious raid and a postponement of the rising to 5 March. Fenian fortunes fared little better on that occasion, as inadequate arms, ineffective leadership, informers and inclement weather conspired to confine the rising to a handful of isolated skirmishes in Kerry, Cork, Tipperary and Dublin. Kelly fled back to England, where he remained undetected until his arrest in Manchester on 11 September, along with another Irish-American conspirator, Timothy Deasy. A week later, a Fenian unit ambushed the prison van in which they were travelling and rescued them, fatally wounding a policeman in the process.

The 'smashing of the van' was the first significant act of Irish revolutionary violence on British soil and was followed in December by the first Fenian bomb explosion in Clerkenwell prison in London which killed twelve people. In October, amid widespread anti-Irish feeling, three men, William Allen, Michael Larkin and Michael O'Brien, were sentenced to death for the policeman's murder. Despite appeals for clemency, they were publicly hanged in Salford prison on 23 November. Their deaths gave the Fenians that priceless political commodity: popular martyrs. As thousands mourned their deaths at home and abroad, the Manchester Martyrs were assumed into the republican pantheon alongside Emmet and Tone.

The abortive 1867 Fenian revolt was more than a mere reaffirmation of the separatist republican faith. It refocused the minds of British politicians on Ireland's unresolved grievances to an unprecedented degree and prompted Liberal leader William Gladstone (1809–98) to pledge himself to the pacification of Ireland, following his general election victory of 1868. Gladstone's objective was to restore the faith of Catholic Ireland in the existing institutions of the Union by redressing Catholic and peasant grievances and undermining support for the militant separatism of the Fenians. His policy was to address immediately two specific Irish grievances which he considered to be at the core of the problem: the privileged position of the Protestant Church of Ireland and the unresolved land issue.

Gladstone moved first to disestablish the Church of Ireland, which by now represented a mere fifth of the Irish population. The 1869 Irish Church Act specified that the Church of Ireland should become a voluntary body from 1871 and disendowed it of its holdings and property. The state grant to the Catholic seminary at Maynooth and the Presbyterian *regium donum* were also abolished. Although all three Churches received capital sums in compensation, no amount of money could alleviate the deep sense of betrayal felt by conservative members of the Church of Ireland, for whom disestablishment represented the first breach of the Union and a portent of the eclipse of Protestant ascendancy in Ireland by the advancing tide of Catholic nationalism.

Gladstone turned next to the thornier issue of Irish land reform. His 1870 Land Act sought to improve landlord–tenant relations by making the 'Ulster custom' statutory throughout the country. This was the first time the government had actively intervened on behalf of Irish tenants and showed Gladstone's willingness to change part of the machinery of Union in order to maintain the overall structure. Though radical in theory, in so far as it implicitly acknowledged the Irish tenant's moral, if not legal, right to his property, the Act had little practical impact on the lives of the peasantry. Indeed, if anything, it increased their impatience for more substantial reforms. The third aspect of Gladstone's positive Irish policy, and the one that proved least effective, was his attempt to redress Irish educational grievances. In 1873 he introduced an Irish University Bill, which sought to establish a new, national, non-sectarian University of Dublin, but the proposal was defeated in the Commons with the help of Irish Liberal MPs. This was a serious defeat for the government which contributed to Gladstone's resignation and eventual replacement by Benjamin Disraeli's Conservative ministry in 1874.

If Fenianism delivered a significant stimulus to the 'greening' of Gladstonian Liberalism, it was also influential in revitalising Irish constitutional nationalism. In May 1870 Isaac Butt (1813–79) formed the Home Government Association in Dublin to agitate for a limited measure of Irish self-government. Butt, a Donegal-born Protestant barrister, began his political career as a Tory unionist but developed a respect for the political integrity, though not the violent methods, of revolutionary nationalists as a result of his experiences as defence counsel to accused Young Irelanders in the 1840s and Fenians in the late 1860s. He saw a constitutional home rule movement as the most effective means of curbing Fenian militancy and protecting his class interests against radical political and social change. As such, Butt's association, which was transformed into the Home Rule League in 1873, was essentially conservative in character, a point underlined by the fact that his proposed federalist arrangement of an Irish parliament, subject to Westminster, but with control over domestic affairs, was far less radical than O'Connell's earlier demand for the repeal of the Union. Butt's movement also lacked the mass appeal of O'Connell's campaign and never gained the wholehearted support of Protestant unionists or Catholic nationalists.

The Irish electorate to which Butt was appealing in the 1870s was a very restricted one, constituting a tiny proportion of the population. Although the Reform Act of 1832 added considerably to the electorate by conferring voting rights on propertied adult males, all women and the majority of the working classes remained disenfranchised. Voter choice was further restricted as a great many constituencies were uncontested. The British electorate was approximately doubled as a result of the 1867 Reform Act, but parallel legislation in Ireland the following year had been far less radical in its effect. The Irish electorate, which was just over 200,000 before the Act (perhaps 13 per cent of adult males), was still below 230,000 in 1880. Futhermore, as the secret ballot was not introduced until 1872, a large proportion of those who had the franchise was still likely to be under strong pressure from a landlord or some other powerful individual to register their vote as he required. To add further to the bias of the electorate towards the wealthy, people who had property in more than one constituency had more than one vote.

Despite these impediments, home rulers scored a number of by-election victories in the early 1870s and won a surprising fifty-nine seats at Westminster in the 1874 general election. While the result indicated the emerging trend of Irish political opinion, these delegates did not as yet constitute a cohesive parliamentary grouping, as their commitment to the home rule issue was complicated by their support for other causes. The parliamentary disparateness of the Irish MPs was exacerbated by Butt's weak leadership, which soon alienated the more radically minded nationalists within the movement. This dissent came to a head in the mid-1870s when two disaffected

MPs, Joseph Biggar, a Belfast Fenian, and Charles Stewart Parnell (1846–91), a Protestant Wicklow landlord, defied their leader and embarked upon a systematic campaign of parliamentary obstruction.

Obstructionism involved delaying the passage of legislation by prolonging debates and proposing numerous amendments and adjournments, all of which was intended to exasperate Westminster politicians into confronting the issue of Irish home rule. Though this combative tactic appalled Butt, a sincere respecter of parliamentary manners, it won Parnell widespread popular support and led to his election as president of the Home Rule Confederation of Great Britain in 1877. Though the effectiveness of obstructionism was reduced by formal changes to the procedural rules of the House in 1881, the tactic yielded significant political dividends for Parnell. It increased his prestige among radical Irish nationalists everywhere, especially in America, where it played an important part in facilitating his acceptance as the leader of this new form of nationalist agitation by the more militant Irish-American republicans.

It was in such circumstances, then, that the man who was to become the greatest leader of nationalist Ireland since O'Connell arrived on the political stage. In many ways, he was an unlikely political messiah, given that his religion and social background were those of the governing class. Yet, the combined influences of his American-born mother's passionate nationalism and his unhappy experiences as a Cambridge undergraduate, where he was made to feel inferior on account of his Irishness, bred in him a fierce patriotism and a corresponding disdain for British parliamentary life and conventions. Within the space of the next decade, this enigmatic yet charismatic figure was to transform irrevocably both the politics of Irish nationalism and the course of Anglo-Irish relations.

6
THE LAND WAR
1879–1882

In the late 1870s an agricultural depression hit Ireland. Wet weather caused the failure of the potato crop in 1877 and 1879, with an inadequate recovery in the intervening year. The worst-affected province was Connacht, which experienced another disastrous potato harvest in 1880. Near-famine conditions prevailed in some parts of the west, notably in County Mayo, where the potato failure had a serious impact upon the rural economy as a whole. The crisis was exacerbated by the fact that Britain was also experiencing an agricultural slump at this time, thus depriving many Connachtmen of their main supplementary source of income as migratory labourers in the harvest fields of England and Scotland.

Unable to pay rent, many smallholders were faced with eviction. The number of evictions trebled between 1877 and 1879, each one evoking grim memories of the Famine. Unlike their predecessors in the 1840s, however, the western peasants were in no mood to capitulate before an impending agricultural catastrophe. Nor were they prepared to relinquish their hard-won post-Famine gains. Organised tenant resistance grew in response to rising evictions, occasionally erupting into violent clashes with landlords, one of which resulted in the murder of Lord Leitrim, a wealthy Donegal landlord, in 1878. As this land agitation gathered momentum, it attracted the involvement of many Fenian activists and sympathisers, one of whom sought to translate this localised agrarian radicalism into a national political movement. His name was Michael Davitt (1846–1906).

Davitt was born to poor Mayo parents who were forced to emigrate to Lancashire in 1851 following their eviction during the Famine. He joined the Fenians while still in his teens and was sentenced to fifteen years' penal servitude in 1870 on a dubious charge relating to arms smuggling. Following his early release in 1877, he met with Parnell to discuss the prospect of political collaboration. Davitt then travelled to America, where he worked closely with John Devoy (1842–1928), the leader of the revolutionary republican organisation Clan na Gael, on a plan to unite the divergent strands of Fenianism, constitutional nationalism and agrarian agitation. The result was the so-called New Departure, whereby Devoy offered Parnell American Fenian support, including financial aid, on condition that he commit himself and the Irish home rule MPs at Westminster to the pursuit of the twin goals of Irish self-government and peasant proprietorship. Though never formally accepted by the Fenian leadership or Parnell, the tacit coalition of Irish agrarian and nationalist interests had a powerful galvanising impact on the inchoate expressions of tenant discontent occurring in the west of Ireland in the spring of 1879.

In April of that year a protest meeting of tenant farmers held in the Mayo village of Irishtown succeeded in forcing a local landlord to reduce his rents and the land war began. Though absent from the Irishtown meeting, Davitt quickly placed himself at the head of this popular agitation by helping to found the National Land League of Mayo in August. In October the Irish National Land League was established with Parnell as president and Davitt as secretary. Parnell had an ambivalent attitude towards the league in so far as he was wary of the large Fenian element in its membership, yet attracted by the possibility of moulding its mass militant support to his own political ends. As for the league itself, its pithy slogan, 'the land for the people', was sufficiently vague to encompass a mixture of moderate and radical aims, some of which were mutually inconsistent: the reduction of rents, the protection of tenants, the abolition of landlordism, the achievement of the three Fs, and, ultimately, the establishment of peasant ownership. Some Land Leaguers contemplated even more fundamental agrarian reforms such as the proposal for the collection of land values by the state, a solution much favoured by the radical Davitt, but far less acceptable to the landlord Parnell.

The Irish land war operated at two levels. At a grassroots level, it comprised a struggle between landowners and peasants; at a political level, it involved a campaign to produce legislation which would ameliorate peasants' grim economic condition. Land League agitation spread rapidly through southern parts of the country and even attracted the sympathy of Protestant farmers in Ulster, though it later came to be perceived by them as a nationalist front. Membership was not confined to impoverished smallholders; large tenant farmers also became actively involved, as did landless labourers, though it had little to offer them in real terms. Nor was the league's base exclusively rural; many shopkeepers and publicans supported tenant resistance, not least because of their economic dependence on the prosperity of farmers. The movement also enjoyed the moral support of the Catholic clergy and won substantial financial backing from Irish-American Fenians.

While the league was officially committed to non-violent, constitutional methods, in practice local activists in some places perpetrated various forms of coercive violence on landlords and their agents, ranging from threatening letters and intimidation to physical assault and murder. The league's most celebrated weapon was the social ostracism of those who took over evicted farms. This tactic was originally christened 'moral Coventry' by Parnell, but a new and more enduring epithet was coined from the surname of the English-born Mayo land agent against whom it was successfully used in the autumn of 1880, Captain Charles Boycott. The co-existence of legal and illegal methods worried Parnell, who was continually faced with the problem of having to decide how far to endorse, ignore or repudiate the activities of league supporters. As the leader of the Irish party at Westminster and president of the Land League in Ireland, he was trying to keep two very different groups working together – a relatively moderate constitutional movement and an increasingly violent agrarian movement with links to Fenianism. It required all his skill to achieve and maintain this difficult balancing act during the 1880s, and in the process avoid alienating possible British support for his political goals of immediate land reform and eventual home rule.

As the frequency of evictions increased, so too did the levels of retaliatory violence. The Liberal government, which was returned to power in 1880 with Gladstone again prime minister, responded by passing coercion legislation and reimprisoning Davitt, who had been freed on ticket-to-leave, in February 1881. Legislation of a more conciliatory kind followed in August in the form of Gladstone's second Land Act. This affirmed the principle of dual ownership by landlord and tenant, granted tenants the right of free sale and introduced arbitration courts to adjudicate in cases of disputed rent increases. In effect, the three Fs were conceded. The Act had only limited success, however, since it made no provision for the thousands of tenants who were in arrears with their rent, or for leaseholders, and it did little to help the smaller tenants of the west, many of whose holdings were too small to support their families.

Rural unrest continued, partly stimulated by Parnell's policy of persuading the Land League to 'test the Act' by taking cases to the land courts, confidently predicting that these test cases would expose the hollowness of Gladstone's legislation. The vehemence of his public opposition to the Act prompted the government to arrest him in October 1881 and incarcerate him in Dublin's Kilmainham jail, where he was later joined by five other leading agitators. One week later the league was suppressed and, in an unprecedented expression of Irish female politicisation, the Ladies' Land League, led by Parnell's sister Anna (1852–1911), assumed control of the campaign in the absence of the male leaders.

This organisation, which was founded by Anna's sister Fanny in New York in October 1880 and launched in Ireland three months later, brought together a remarkable group of radical female activists in what was the first movement of its kind to emerge in Ireland. Initially, the women concentrated their energies on providing moral and material support for evicted families, but after the removal of the male leadership, Anna, who espoused a more radical politics than her brother, was in favour of more extreme forms of civil disobedience, including an all-out rent strike. However, the apathetic rural response to this proposal, coupled with her brother's curt dismissal of her on his release from prison in May 1882, left her rightly sceptical about the true revolutionary potential of the league, which she later derided as 'a great sham'. The Ladies' Land League was eventually dissolved in August 1882.

Meanwhile, the war escalated during the winter of 1881–82. Parnell, after much persuasion by his imprisoned colleagues, issued, as a temporary tactic, a fruitless 'no-rent' manifesto from prison, directing tenants to begin a rent strike. The government responded by intensifying its coercive measures, which in turn provoked further agrarian outrages. With rural anarchy looming, Gladstone and Parnell came to a mutual recognition of the need for compromise. The result was the Kilmainham 'Treaty' negotiated in April 1882. Gladstone agreed to amend the terms of the 1881 Land Act to include tenants in arrears and leaseholders, in return for which he received assurances from Parnell that he would use his influence to bring about an end to rural lawlessness and support Liberal reforms. Though the murder of Lord Frederick Cavendish, the new Irish chief secretary, and his under-secretary, Thomas Burke, by a republican splinter group in Dublin's Phoenix Park on 6 May overshadowed the announcement of the agreement, the Kilmainham accord effectively brought the land war to an end. Although agrarian agitation continued on a sporadic basis throughout the following two decades, tenant disaffection was never again so massively or so effectively mobilised.

The effects of the land war were numerous and far-reaching. It brought about a major change in the Irish landholding system by beginning the process of peasant ownership, which was continued by further Land Acts over the next twenty years, culminating in the Wyndham Act of 1903 (amended in 1909). By 1914, two-thirds of Irish farmers owned their land. Over the following fifty years, this massive transfer of land led to a great reduction in the number of traditional landlords, while, at the same time, other changes would lead to the virtual disappearance of the class of landless farm labourers. Yet 'the fall of feudalism', as Davitt famously termed it, did not alter the *nature* of landholding in Ireland, since land was consolidated in the hands of the owners as a result of the land war, not redistributed. This meant that the main beneficiaries of the crisis were the propertied classes, especially the strong farmers, a fact which underlines the socially conservative nature of the tenurial reforms. Nor did the land war bring about the desired Irish agricultural miracle, since the Land Acts were political in their ends, not economic. Thus, Irish farming remained inefficient and uncompetitive after the land reforms, and those who had been landless beforehand benefited little or nothing from the whole process. In one sense, their position was even worse, since they now had little chance of making common cause with the tenant farmers, who were largely satisfied by the new arrangements.

The land war established Parnell as the dominant figure on the Irish political landscape. His skilful manipulation of the potentially destructive forces unleashed by the war gave him a popular appeal of regal proportions, as reflected in his metaphorical enthronement as 'the uncrowned king of Ireland', a title which had formerly been applied to O'Connell. He had adroitly walked the tightrope between the poles of constitutional and revolutionary agitation and managed to keep his political balance. Not only this, but his successful conjunction of nationalist and agrarian issues revitalised the home rule movement and gave it a crucially important social base among the Irish tenantry. Yet, as rural agitation abated and Catholic Ireland contemplated the significance of his – and its – victory in the summer of 1882, Parnell's ultimate political goal of Irish home rule lay as far away as ever. It was to the pursuit of this goal that he now turned, vigorously reasserting the primacy of constitutional agitation over agrarian activism.

7

THE HOME RULE CONTROVERSY
1882–1893

Parnell's shift from agrarian to political agitation was formally marked by the establishment of the Irish National League which replaced the Land League in October 1882. This organisation had as its primary objective the achievement of national self-government by constitutional means, with land law reform relegated to a list of subsidiary aims. Over the next three years the National League became a highly efficient and disciplined political machine which Parnell used to transform his parliamentary following into the first modern Irish political party, and home rule into a national movement.

The third Reform Act of 1884 was an important contributory factor in this transformation. This Act increased the Irish electorate from about 230,000 to around 740,000, thereby adding more than half a million men to the voting register. This was still only about half of the adult male population, and it did not include any women, but at least it meant that the great majority of male householders, rich and poor, rural and urban, received the vote. Many of these new voters, especially the small farmers and labourers, flocked to Parnell's party which by 1885 had come to embody the political aspirations of Catholic nationalist Ireland. Parnell himself gave eloquent expression to these aspirations in one of his most famous speeches, delivered in Cork in January 1885, when he proclaimed that

no man has the right to fix the boundary to the march of a nation. No man has a right to say to his country, 'thus far shalt thou go and no further', and we have never attempted to fix the *ne plus ultra* to the progress of Ireland's nationhood, and we never shall.

At Westminster Parnell maintained an independent opposition to both major parties, while simultaneously remaining open to the possibility of a tactical alliance with any faction which might further his cause of Irish legislative independence. Such an opportunity presented itself in June 1885 when Parnellites combined with Conservatives to defeat Gladstone's Liberal government in a Commons budget vote, after which the Conservative Lord Salisbury (1830–1903) formed a caretaker administration, pending a December general election. One significant piece of Irish land purchase legislation emerged during this period, the 1885 Ashbourne Act, which allowed tenants to borrow the full amount of the purchase price of their holdings. Attempts to extract a pre-election commitment to Irish home rule from either Salisbury or Gladstone proved fruitless, however, as both leaders maintained a studied vagueness on the issue. In the end Parnell came out in favour of the Tories, encouraged by their recent conciliatory Irish policies, and with memories of Liberal coercion still fresh in his mind.

The result of the 1885 election could hardly have been more

momentous for nationalist Ireland. In what was essentially a referendum on home rule, Parnellites won an astonishing eighty-six seats (including one in Liverpool), Irish Liberal representation disappeared completely, and Irish Conservatives were reduced to a rump of sixteen pro-Union MPs overwhelmingly concentrated in the north-eastern part of Ulster. Home rulers now held the balance of power at Westminster between the Liberals with 335 seats and Conservatives with 249. With British political minds focused intensely on the Irish question, the Liberal leader's son, Herbert, suddenly announced on 17 December that his father had been 'converted' to the principle of home rule for Ireland. While there was obviously an element of political calculation in Gladstone's decision, it also contained a strong measure of that moral conviction which had shown itself in his 1869 Church Act. Furthermore, the 1885 general election had proved to him that a large majority of the Irish people favoured home rule and was not likely to be persuaded otherwise. On that judgement, home rule must come sooner or later. But to seek to refine the machinery of Union, as Gladstone had done in his earlier administrations, was one thing; to suggest that the whole structure might be dismantled, quite another.

Gladstone's political conversion precipitated a dramatic and durable realignment of forces within the Anglo-Irish political nexus. Whereas Parnellites gratefully embraced the Liberals and secured Gladstone's appointment as prime minister for a third time in February 1886, Conservatives reaffirmed their commitment to maintaining the integrity of the Union. In an age of empire, Ireland became an issue upon which they could unite, as Salisbury's succinct statement confirmed: 'Ireland must be kept, like India, at all hazards; by persuasion, if possible; if not, by force.' Some English Tories adopted a more belligerent unionist stance, notably Lord Randolph Churchill

(1849–95), father of Sir Winston, an ambitious young Conservative with leadership aspirations. He saw in the developing crisis an opportunity for political self-advancement and decided that if Gladstone tried to introduce Irish home rule, 'the Orange card would be the one to play'.

Playing the Orange card meant tactically exploiting Ulster Protestant opposition to rule by a Dublin parliament dominated by Catholic nationalists. As the nationalist demand for legislative independence grew ever more vociferous in the 1880s, so too did resistance to home rule among Protestant Conservatives in Ulster, the only province where they were in a majority. Ulster Protestant attachment to the Union was rooted in a complex amalgam of factors. In earlier times, the Protestants of Ulster, far from resisting the cause of Irish self-government, had largely spearheaded the independence movement. But a great deal had changed since the turn of the century. Emancipation ensured that the great majority of Irish MPS was now Catholic, and this would certainly remain the case in any future Irish parliament. The 1869 Irish Church Act, which came into effect in 1871, removed the grievance against the privileged position of the Church of Ireland which Presbyterians and other non-conformists had shared with Catholics. Moreover, at a time when monarchy and empire were greatly in vogue, Ulster Protestants' distinct sense of cultural identity was overlaid by an emotional attachment to the trappings and traditions of the British crown, which they came to perceive as part of their common British inheritance.

This loyalism was further underpinned by an economic faith in the material benefits of the empire. By the late nineteenth century north-east Ulster had developed into the most prosperous part of Ireland, its economy founded on the linen, shipbuilding and engineering industries of Belfast and its hinterland. This industrial wealth, which was concentrated in

Protestant hands, was highly dependent upon Britain and the empire for its raw materials and markets. Hence, many Ulster businessmen and workers feared that home rule would jeopardise their economic prosperity and imagined a bleak future where, as Conservative MP Arthur Balfour prophesied in 1893, 'the wealthy, the orderly, the industrious, the enterprising portion of Ireland' would be dominated by the 'less orderly, less industrious, less enterprising and less law-abiding' portion.

Deep-seated religious anxieties also played a part in Ulster's opposition to home rule. Undimmed historical memories of the massacres of Protestants in 1641 and 1798 meant that the fear of popery was never far from the Ulster Protestant mind. More recently, the widespread Protestant unease generated by the disestablishment of the Church of Ireland was deepened by the unmistakably Catholic character of agrarian and Parnellite agitation, all of which led many Ulster Protestants to conclude that home rule would mean Rome rule. Whereas class, regional and denominational divisions had conspired to divide Ulster Protestants heretofore, the gravity of the situation in the mid-1880s forced disparate groups to cohere into a united anti-home-rule movement, which formed the basis for the formal political organisation known as Ulster unionism.

In January 1886 Belfast Conservatives formed the Ulster Loyalist Anti-Repeal Union to co-ordinate a campaign of resistance to home rule. They were joined in protest by members of the Orange Order which underwent a popular revival in the early 1880s and received an influx of members from all social classes. What was once an almost exclusively working-class body was now transformed into an organisation to which lords, labourers and landed gentry belonged. A key figure in both organisations was Edward Saunderson (1837–1906), Tory MP for North Armagh, who arranged a series of public meetings in early 1886 to stir popular Protestant opposition. The meetings culminated in a massive gathering in Belfast's Ulster Hall on 22 February at which Churchill pledged that 'Ulster at the proper moment will resort to the supreme arbitrament of force', and gave unionism its enduring rallying cry: 'Ulster will fight and Ulster will be right.'

Such inflammatory sentiments inevitably heightened sectarian tension in the city and contributed to the eruption of rioting in June. In the longer term, Churchill's intervention laid the foundation for an alliance between unionists in Britain and Ulster which was to have far-reaching implications for future Anglo-Irish relations. His militant theme was quickly taken up by Saunderson, who was instrumental in moulding Ulster Conservative MPs at Westminster into a distinct parliamentary grouping which vehemently opposed Gladstone's first Home Rule Bill, introduced in the Commons on 8 April 1886.

The Bill proposed the establishment of a two-tier Dublin parliament which would have responsibility for a limited range of domestic Irish affairs, with the imperial parliament retaining control over such matters as foreign policy, trade and defence. Irish representation at Westminster would cease, though the country would continue to contribute to imperial expenditure. There were close parallels with the Austro-Hungarian *Ausgleich* of 1867. British Conservatives joined Ulster unionists in opposing the Bill, while Parnell and his party welcomed it as a modest devolutionary measure which could be extended at a later date. But the most decisive opposition originated from within Gladstone's own party.

Liberal dissent came from two main factions, one led by the Whig Lord Hartington (1833–1908), the other by the radical Joseph Chamberlain (1836–1914). Both men saw in Irish home rule the seeds of separatism and the disintegration of the empire. When, on 8 June, a vote was taken, ninety-three Liberals voted against the government and the Bill was defeated by thirty votes. A historic opportunity to resolve the Irish question had been squandered and Gladstone's prophetic words went unheeded: 'Ireland stands at your bar expectant, hopeful, almost suppliant . . . Think, I beseech you, think well, think wisely, think, not for the moment, but for the years that are to come, before you reject this bill.'

He immediately called an election in which Irish home rule was the central issue. His devolutionary plans were comprehensively rejected by the English electorate, however, though Wales and Scotland returned home rule majorities. The Conservatives returned to power, supported by the dissident Liberals, now reconstituted as the Liberal Unionist Party. Salisbury's government remained in office until 1892, during which time Irish home rule languished with the Liberal–Parnellite alliance on the opposition benches.

The events of 1885–86 had a lasting significance for politics in Ireland, north and south. Not only did these years witness the birth of modern Irish political parties, they also established the basic framework within which the territorial and constitutional conflicts which culminated in the partition of the island in 1920 were played out. The new geographic and demographic contours of Irish democracy were revealed, as the clear emergence of two distinct, mutually antagonistic movements, nationalism and unionism, polarised Irish politics along religious grounds. From now on denominational affiliation became the key determinant of political allegiance, obscuring social, class and regional differences. With very few exceptions, to be Catholic in Ireland was to be nationalist, to be Protestant, unionist. Ironically, Parnell was one of those few exceptions.

This correlation between religion and politics was particularly intense in Ulster because of the evenly divided nature of the Protestant/unionist Catholic/nationalist split there, which became visible in the mid-1880s and changed little in the following two decades. Thus, the roots of the modern Ulster problem are deeply embedded in the political developments of 1885–86. In one important respect, however, the nineteenth-century debates over Ireland's future were very different from those which would take place in the twentieth. No significant political figure on either side of the controversy proposed any kind of territorial division between Catholic and Protestant parts of the country. Inside or outside the Union, all tacitly agreed that Ireland should remain an integrated whole.

The late 1880s was a time of mixed political and personal fortunes for Parnell. With home rule postponed indefinitely, nationalist attention in Ireland reverted to the issue of land reform. Agrarian agitation was renewed in the autumn of 1886 in the form of the Plan of Campaign, whereby tenants on various estates organised a series of co-ordinated rent strikes. Though the campaign was spearheaded by two of his acolytes, Parnell himself disapproved of it, seeing it as a distraction from the larger political objective of self-government. Meanwhile, a series of articles appeared in *The Times* in the spring of 1887 accusing Parnell of Fenian conspiracy and purporting to show that he had condoned the Phoenix Park murders of 1882. The judicial commission which was set up to inquire into the affair eventually exonerated him and exposed the allegations as false in a report published in February 1890. Parnell had little time to savour this public vindication of his political integrity, however, as a much graver crisis was already upon him.

In December 1889 Captain William O'Shea filed a petition for divorce from his wife, Katharine, naming Parnell as co-respondent. The couple had been lovers since 1880 and had lived together, with O'Shea's knowledge, since 1886. When the case came to court in November 1890 Parnell did not contest the divorce because he wanted to marry Katharine. Consequently, the evidence submitted about his private life went unchallenged. Victorian society on both sides of the Irish Sea was scandalised by the lurid revelations which emerged, and Parnell's reputation was seriously damaged.

Moral outrage was especially strong among English non-conformists, who comprised the bedrock of Liberal support in Britain. A dismayed Gladstone, mindful of the destructive impact the adulterous revelations would have on the Liberal vote and therefore on the home rule cause, realised that if Parnell did not resign, his own leadership would become un-tenable and home rule would be jeopardised. However, his request that Parnell relinquish his party leadership, even tem-porarily, in order to save the Liberal alliance met with an in-transigent response. Parnell denounced Gladstone, thus jettisoning the alliance. The Irish leader's stubbornness led in turn to an acrimonious and deeply damaging split within his own parliamentary party, the majority of whom rejected him in order to preserve the alliance.

Parnell responded by appealing to the people who had once acclaimed him as their king. He spent much of 1891 in Ireland, campaigning intensively on behalf of Parnellite candidates in by-elections in North Kilkenny, North Sligo and Carlow. The campaigns were among the most acrimonious in living memory, as Parnellites and anti-Parnellites indulged in corus-cating verbal attacks on each other, some of which spilled over into violence. Parnellites insisted that loyalty to their leader took precedence over the dictates of British politicians, reli-gious morality and public opinion; anti-Parnellites, supported by the Catholic hierarchy, condemned him as a moral outcast who was unfit to be leader. Parnell's candidates lost all three by-elections. In June he married his beloved Katharine, despite intense condemnation from the Catholic hierarchy and the

Dublin media, most of which had now deserted him. Exhausted and in ill health, Parnell went home to Brighton where he died unexpectedly on 6 October 1891, aged forty-five, with Katharine at his side. Five days later, over two hundred thousand mourners lined the streets of Dublin to honour the man who had embodied their dream of political autonomy and dignified the quest to realise it. In the nation as a whole a collective sense of guilt seemed to prevail, as people came to terms with the premature death of Ireland's uncrowned king.

Parnell's influence on Irish nationalism was both divisive and unifying. His immediate legacy was a bitterly divided Irish Parliamentary Party which remained fragmented until 1900 when it was reunited under John Redmond (1856–1918). At a more fundamental level, however, Parnell forged a powerful sense of Irish nationhood and bequeathed a potent legacy of expectation to the next generation of Irish nationalists, the great majority of whom carried on the tradition of parliamentary agitation for home rule which he so brilliantly revitalised.

The Irish Parliamentary Party, as will be seen, eventually recovered from the traumas of the 1890s, and by 1914 had succeeded in placing home rule on the statute book, only to have its implementation deferred by the outbreak of the First World War. In the ensuing hiatus, the Parnellite legacy was spectacularly and unexpectedly eclipsed by the minority Fenian tradition of non-constitutional, revolutionary nationalism, which achieved its apotheosis in the 1916 rising and its aftermath. By then Parnell's fate had assumed legendary proportions in the Irish historical consciousness, his memory lionised by writers like W.B. Yeats and James Joyce, who saw in his demise a tragedy of epic dimensions and mythologised him as a prophet betrayed by craven minds.

It was also Parnell's achievement to establish the issue of Irish home rule at the centre of *British* politics, and its importance did not end with his death. Gladstone was returned to power in 1892 with home rule high on his legislative agenda, despite the fact that the Irish Parliamentary Party was now hopelessly split between anti-Parnellites, who were in the great majority, and Parnellites. A second Home Rule Bill was introduced early in 1893 with somewhat different provisions from its predecessor, including the retention of Irish MPs at Westminster. It received a small Commons majority in September but was overwhelmingly rejected by the large unionist majority in the Lords a week later. In March 1894 Gladstone, aged eighty-four, resigned as prime minister and was succeeded by the imperialist Lord Rosebery (1847–1929). When Rosebery's ministry was replaced by a Conservative-dominated government in 1895, a decade of Tory rule began, during which time home rule was, in Salisbury's words, left to sleep 'the sleep of the unjust'.

8

THE NATIONALIST REVIVAL
1894–1912

Gladstone's retirement in 1894 marked the end of an era in Anglo-Irish politics. Without his energy and enthusiasm, the alliance between the Liberal and Irish parties began to disintegrate. The Liberals, increasingly beset by internal splits and schisms, lost much of their commitment to the Irish cause, while the Irish Parliamentary Party ended the century in a weak and fragmented state. The responsibility for solving the Irish problem now passed to the Conservatives, who were in power from 1895 to 1905. For much of this period the Tories adopted a conciliatory approach towards Ireland known as 'constructive unionism' or, more revealingly, 'killing home rule with kindness'. As this phrase suggests, the government hoped to undermine nationalist support for home rule by ameliorating some of the country's most pressing social and economic ills. Constructive unionism also represented a final attempt by the defenders of the Irish propertied classes, which had dominated landed wealth since the eighteenth century, to devise a settlement which would preserve something of their power and privilege. Its eventual failure sealed the fate of the Anglo-Irish Protestant ascendancy class as a political force in Irish life, leaving them, like their big houses, vulnerably isolated in a changing social and political landscape.

The first exponent of constructive unionism was Arthur Balfour (1848–1930), Irish chief secretary from 1887 to 1891. Whereas Gladstone saw legislative independence as the panacea for Irish unrest, Balfour proposed a dual policy of resolute government and radical reform, declaring: 'I shall be as ruthless as Cromwell in enforcing obedience to the law, but at the same time I shall be as radical as any reformer in redressing grievances and especially in removing every cause of complaint in regard to the land.' The first fruits of his pledge were the Irish Land Acts of 1887, 1888 and 1891, all of which he successfully piloted through parliament. These Acts sought to extend the land purchase schemes of previous governments stretching back to 1869 by encouraging landlords to sell, and tenants to buy, their farms, while sometimes providing a certain amount of public money to lubricate the deals. In 1891 Balfour also established the Congested Districts Board to ameliorate the particular economic problems of the west and south through the promotion of such measures as farm modernisation and local cottage industry.

Gerald Balfour, chief secretary of Ireland from 1895 to 1900, continued his brother's progressive economic policies by increasing the amount of money available for land purchase and overseeing the Local Government Act of 1898. The democratic reforms carried out under this Act brought about such a dramatic transfer of power from unionists to nationalists at a district council level that the result was a form of local home rule. Five years later, the policy of constructive unionism culminated in the Wyndham Land Act, which effectively completed the process of creating a peasant proprietorship and abolishing landlordism with the tacit consent of the beleaguered landowning class. As a result, this Act did much to determine the social composition of twentieth-century rural Ireland.

Though it brought about several far-reaching social and economic changes, constructive unionism ultimately failed to silence the nationalist demand for home rule. Whatever their material benefits, land purchase schemes and local government reforms were no substitute for legislative autonomy, the desire for which had, if anything, grown more intense during ten years of Tory rule. The nationalist revival of this period came not from the faction-ridden home rulers, but from extra-parliamentary quarters. The late nineteenth and early twentieth centuries witnessed the burgeoning of a vibrant Irish cultural nationalism and the revitalisation of a moribund revolutionary separatism, both of which challenged the hegemony of constitutional nationalism, the former implicitly, the latter explicitly. The dividing line between cultural and political activism faded as intellectuals and revolutionaries came together in a plethora of literary and cultural societies, all seeking to forge a new spirit of Irishness and engender a popular reawakening of national consciousness. The result was a potent, mutually reinforcing bond between culture and politics, the nature of which was succinctly encapsulated in the advice given to the young W.B. Yeats (1865–1939) by the veteran Fenian John O'Leary: 'There is no great literature without nationality, no nationality without literature.'

Yeats himself was by far the most influential proponent of what came to be known as the Irish literary revival. As poet, dramatist, critic and polemicist, he spearheaded the search for appropriate artistic forms to express a modern but distinctively

Irish cultural identity. He founded the National Literary Society in Dublin in 1892 and seven years later was instrumental in establishing a national theatre in Dublin which became the Abbey Theatre in 1904. The rediscovery and restoration of Ireland's indigenous Gaelic heritage, especially the rich language and folklore of peasant life, lay at the heart of this cultural enterprise. Ironically, Yeats himself knew little Gaelic, nor was it the first language of other prominent revivalists such as George Moore, Lady Augusta Gregory and John Millington Synge, most of whom came from Anglo-Irish Protestant backgrounds. Yet, through their poetry, plays, novels and short stories, they created a romanticised, idealised version of Irish community and tradition which restored the nation's cultural self-respect and energised the struggle for political independence.

Irish cultural nationalism had its roots in the 1880s. One of the first and most popular manifestations of this phenomenon was the Gaelic Athletic Association, a national sporting organisation founded in 1884 with the aim of promoting native Irish sports such as hurling and Gaelic football. The GAA was an essentially rural movement with a distinctly anti-English sporting bias which made it attractive to more politically minded Irish separatists in the Fenian movement. The association consequently became a recruiting ground for militant nationalists, two thousand of whom formed a guard of honour at Parnell's funeral, bearing hurling sticks. This fusion of cultural and political nationalism was also a feature of the Gaelic League, in many ways the urban counterpart of the GAA. The league was founded by Douglas Hyde (1860–1949) and Eoin MacNeill (1867–1945) in 1893 for the specific purpose of reviving Irish as a national spoken language. Hyde, a Protestant scholar who became the first president of Ireland in 1938, saw language revival as the first step towards the 'de-anglicization' of the nation and the recovery of a distinct sense of Irish nationality.

Like the GAA, the league began as a non-political organisation, but quickly assumed a nationalist character and came under the formal political influence of the IRB in 1915, a move which prompted Hyde's resignation. Many Gaelic Leaguers went on to participate in the 1916 Easter Rising, including Patrick Pearse (1879–1916), whose vision of an Ireland 'not free merely, but Gaelic as well; not Gaelic merely, but free as well' was heavily influenced by the league's ethos.

Two events in the closing years of the century provided cultural and political separatists with a timely focus for the expression of their nationalist feeling: the centenary celebrations of the 1798 rising and the South African Boer War (1899–1902). IRB members and cultural activists were prominent in the nationwide establishment of 1798 commemorative committees, many of which also contained Irish MPs. Indeed, there was a rich irony in the spectacle of modern Irish constitutional nationalists commemorating the violent deeds of their militant republican ancestors. Those late-Victorian politicians might even have reflected that the government against which the 1798 rebels had taken arms was an Irish one with powers remarkably similar to those for which latter-day home rulers were clamouring.

The centenary celebrations also cast Ireland's contemporary ideological divisions into stark relief. While nationalists celebrated in 1898, northern unionists were hostile, since Tone's ideal of uniting Protestant, Catholic and Dissenter in an independent Irish republic was no longer one with which they could empathise. There was, therefore, a sad irony in the fact that the largely Presbyterian 1798 rising in Antrim and Down was commemorated mainly by Catholics in 1898, while alienated Presbyterians stayed away.

The 1798 centenary was also celebrated thousands of miles away by Irish nationalists in South Africa, many of whom were workers in the country's gold mines. When war broke out in October 1899, many of these men saw in the Boer cause a reflection of their own anti-imperial struggle. In Ireland, the South African war was a matter of considerable controversy. Whereas many advanced nationalists saw in the conflict yet another manifestation of the cloven hoof of British imperialism, other Irishmen were recruited into the British army in substantial numbers.

Among those who organised the Johannesburg celebrations was Arthur Griffith (1871–1922), a young Dublin journalist and IRB member who, on his return to Ireland, recognised the need for a national organisation to co-ordinate the activities of the disparate nationalist groups, separatist and otherwise, then flourishing. The result was the Sinn Féin League established in 1907 and reconstituted as a national organisation in 1908 as Sinn Féin, meaning 'ourselves'.

Sinn Féin's central objective was the re-establishment, by non-violent means, of an independent Irish parliament in Dublin under the British crown. Griffith recommended that Irish nationalists withdraw from Westminster, constitute themselves as an Irish government and implement policies of economic protectionism, which he supposed would encourage industrial development. Such radicalism was obviously at odds with the policy of the Irish Parliamentary Party, whose support base was targeted by the new movement. Griffith's policies failed to win popular support, however, and Sinn Féin remained a marginal force in Irish politics until its sudden resurgence after the 1916 rising. A key factor in its marginalisation was Griffith's failure to capture the middle ground between constitutional nationalism and militant republicanism, both of which were undergoing a revitalisation at this time. On the republican side, some of the more militant Sinn Féin members found Griffith's idea of a dual monarchy on the Austro-Hungarian model too conservative and looked instead to a revival of the dormant IRB. Inspired by the return to Ireland in 1907 of the veteran Fenian Tom Clarke, they set about recruiting energetic new members and renewing the revolutionary ethos of the organisation. Yet, for all its internal changes, the IRB remained a secret, underground movement which had little impact upon politics at a popular level at this time. Instead, it was to the reunited Irish Parliamentary Party at Westminster that the majority of Irish nationalists looked when the issue of home rule returned to the top of the Liberal agenda in 1910.

In the closing years of the nineteenth century the Irish Parliamentary Party, which had been deeply divided since the Parnell split in 1890, began to heal its divisions. How far this process of reconciliation may be attributed to the recollection of 1798 is arguable, but in 1900 the two factions reunited under the leadership of the erstwhile Parnellite, John Redmond. The new leader was a Wicklow landlord who had sat for Waterford City since a hotly contested election battle against Michael Davitt in 1892. Redmond, however, would never attain the unrivalled authority which O'Connell and Parnell possessed in their heydays, and he was at times seriously challenged by other nationalist politicians who felt that their leadership credentials were at least as good as his.

The 1906 general election returned the Liberals to power with a parliamentary majority so large that it made them independent of the Irish Parliamentary Party. However, the new Liberal prime minister, Sir Henry Campbell-Bannerman (1836–1908), was sympathetic to nationalists' demands and pledged himself to a gradualist devolutionary policy. Thus, the Tory approach of 'killing home rule with kindness' gave way to the Liberal policy of conceding 'home rule by instalments'. The first instalment was offered in 1907 when the government proposed the establishment of an Irish Council which would grant Dublin a measure of administrative, but not legislative, autonomy. However, this compromise solution proved wholly unacceptable to Irish nationalists and was rejected by Redmond and his party. Despite this setback, the Liberal alliance went on to achieve more modest reforms in the areas of Irish housing and education until 1909, when the House of Lords' rejection of the reforming budget drawn up by the chancellor, David Lloyd George (1863–1945), precipitated a constitutional crisis and led to two general elections in 1910.

The elections wiped out the Liberal majority, and left the Irish nationalists, with eighty-two MPs, again holding the balance of power. Redmond's strategy was to trade Irish parliamentary support for a public commitment from the new Liberal leader, Herbert Asquith (1852–1928), that he would introduce a Home Rule Bill. Redmond's cause was boosted in 1911, when the continuing conflict between the Commons and the Lords culminated in the passing of the Parliament Act, which drastically reduced the power of the Lords to veto legislation to a maximum of two years, after which time it would automatically receive the royal assent. This landmark Act made the implementation of Irish home rule virtually inevitable, if the Liberals remained in government. This inevitability came a step closer in April 1912, when Asquith brought the third Home Rule Bill before the Commons. The Bill resembled Gladstone's 1893 proposals in its provision for a two-tier Irish legislature under the overall control of Westminster. Irish MPs would continue to attend Westminster, but their number would be reduced to forty-two. After years of desert wanderings, Irish nationalists seemed finally within sight of the promised land. But as the bright vista of self-government opened up before them, the daunting obstacle of Protestant Ulster suddenly loomed back into view, blocking the path to freedom.

While the home rule issue dominated Anglo-Irish politics during the late nineteenth and early twentieth centuries, this period also saw the emergence of other political forces, notably the labour and suffrage movements. The labour movement in Britain was spearheaded by James Keir Hardie, who formed the Independent Labour Party in 1893 and was elected chairman of the first parliamentary Labour Party in 1906. The first Irish socialist party was formed in Dublin in 1896 by James Connolly (1868–1916), whose political vision was of an independent socialist republic. At the beginning of the twentieth century, however, the Irish labour movement was weak and numerically small, being based mainly on craft unions and with its greatest strength among the Belfast Protestant working class.

In January 1907 Liverpool-born trade unionist James Larkin (1876–1947) arrived in Belfast as organiser for the National Union of Dock Labourers. Within months he had successfully unionised most of the unskilled workers, both Protestant and Catholic. Then in May a major dispute began between dock workers and their employers over the right to trade union membership. The strike paralysed the city until August, and while it was eventually broken and the dockers defeated, Larkin had for a short time succeeded in bridging the sectarian and political divide between Belfast workers. This solidarity was not to last, however, and Protestant and Catholic employees soon reverted to their traditional political allegiances.

In December 1908 Larkin founded the Irish Transport and General Workers' Union (ITGWU) in Dublin, which soon became a dynamic force in the development of the Irish labour movement. The industrial unrest which affected much of Europe in the pre-war years also reached Ireland. In Dublin most working-class men were unskilled 'casuals' who were poorly paid and lived in dreadful slum tenements where mal-nutrition, disease and high mortality rates were rife. A series of strikes organised by Larkin and Connolly demanding better conditions for workers and recognition for the ITGWU culminated in the lock-out of some 25,000 workers by over 400 Dublin employers in September 1913. There followed a bitter five-month struggle between labour and capital, which united workers, intellectuals and militant nationalists against employers, the Catholic hierarchy and the mainly middle-class Irish Parliamentary Party. The struggle ended in victory for the employers when the strikers were forced back to work in January and February 1914. While this outcome represented a major blow to the development of socialism in Ireland, the lock-out also acted as a stimulus to the dynamic fusion of nationalism and socialism, which culminated in Connolly's small Irish Citizen Army taking part in the 1916 rising.

One of the many democratising measures which Connolly supported was the extension of the franchise to women in Ireland and Britain. The two decades between the second and third Home Rule Bills witnessed the rise of militant women's suffrage movements in both countries. Prior to this, a small number of women's rights activists had campaigned for educational and political reforms with limited success. A new model presented itself in 1903 when Emmeline Pankhurst and her daughters established the Women's Social and Political Union in Manchester. This organisation introduced the concept of militant action into the English suffrage campaign and its influence soon spread to Ireland, where the Irish Women's Franchise League was founded by Hanna Sheehy-Skeffington (1877–1946) and Margaret Cousins in 1908.

The league was a non-party association which aimed to obtain the parliamentary vote for Irish women on the same terms as men. Proclaiming 'suffrage first before all else!', it pressurised Irish Parliamentary Party MPs to insist on the inclusion of a women's suffrage clause in the 1912 Home Rule Bill. Redmond consistently opposed the suffragists' demands, however, as did Asquith, Edward Carson and Andrew Bonar Law. The activists' subsequent resort to militant tactics shocked many observers. In June 1912 eight members of the Irish Women's Franchise League, including Hanna Sheehy-Skeffington, were arrested for breaking windows in government buildings in Dublin Castle. This was followed by the arrest and imprisonment of two English suffragettes for violent demonstration during Asquith's visit to Dublin in July. Suffrage militancy continued over the next two years, yet failed to win concessions. This failure was compounded by the outbreak of war in 1914, which saw suffragist unity give way to divergent strands of political activity. Some women supported the war effort, others were pacifists, while yet others committed themselves to the struggle for Irish independence.

A degree of solidarity between the various women's groups was restored in the aftermath of the 1916 rising, which proclaimed the equal citizenship of Irish men and women. Less than two years later, in February 1918, the Representation of the People Act granted the vote to most women over thirty years of age, despite the continuing reservations of some Ulster Unionists at Westminster. In the 1918 general election Sinn Féin's Constance Markievicz (1868–1927) became the first female MP elected to the British parliament, but did not take up her seat. Instead she was appointed minister for labour in the first Dáil Éireann in January 1919. Three years later, following a heated debate which revealed a formidable degree of chauvinism among Irish male politicians, the Irish Free State constitution of 1922 granted the right to vote to all men and women over the age of twenty-one. Women in Northern Ireland and Britain had to wait until 1928 to be similarly enfranchised.

9
ULSTER AND HOME RULE
1905–1914

For Ulster unionists the period between the second and third Home Rule Bills was a time of uneasy calm punctuated by moments of heightened tension. The Lords' rejection of Gladstone's 1893 Bill and the subsequent defeat of the Liberals in the 1895 election allayed immediate unionist anxieties, but left endemic Protestant fears intact. The home rule tiger was not dead but sleeping, so vigilance, fortitude and solidarity needed to be maintained. But whereas the minority southern unionist community began a slow, painful process of *rapprochement* with the emergent Catholic nationalist order as the 1900s unfolded, Ulster Protestants retreated into a robust insularity, fortified by their sense of cultural and religious separateness.

This psychological isolationism manifested itself politically in a continuing determination to maintain Protestant ascendancy in Ulster by all means necessary. The slogan of the

1880s still expressed the essence of unionist resistance to an independent Irish parliament: 'home rule is Rome rule'. The first crisis of the new century occurred in 1904–5 when some southern unionist landlords collaborated with Conservative government officials in the formulation of a devolutionary scheme for Ireland. The move alarmed Ulster unionists, who perceived the proposals as a disguised form of home rule. They responded by forming the defensive Ulster Unionist Council in March 1905, an umbrella organisation which embraced MPs, Orangemen, landowners and businessmen. But the real crisis lay some years in the future.

Unionist apprehensions resurfaced when the outcry caused by Lloyd George's 1909 budget led to a general election at which Irish nationalists were able to extract a commitment to home rule from Asquith. Memories of the 1880s were revived as Redmond tried to play Parnell's part by using his party's balance of power as a bargaining card in negotiations with the Liberals. When Asquith curbed the Lords' veto in 1911 and signalled his intention to introduce a third Home Rule Bill, unionist alarm reached fever pitch. The Ulster Unionist Council stepped up its campaign of resistance by organising unionist clubs in Ulster and mobilising anti-home-rule opinion in Ireland and Britain. Mass rallies were organised, at which the new hardline leaders of Ulster loyalism, Edward Carson (1854–1935), a Dublin-born lawyer and MP for Dublin University who became leader of the Irish unionist MPs at Westminster in 1910, and James Craig (1871–1940), the son of a millionaire Ulster Presbyterian whiskey distiller, prophesied militant action if home rule was introduced.

Carson's fundamental political objective was to preserve the whole of Ireland from home rule. His leadership of the Ulster unionists was predicated on the belief that if home rule could be resisted by Ulster, then it could not be applied to the rest of

Ireland. His eventual acceptance of a partitionist compromise was arrived at reluctantly, after he realised that all of Ireland could not be saved from what he regarded as 'the most nefarious conspiracy that has ever been hatched against a free people'. Craig's primary concern, on the other hand, was to preserve the position of Protestant Ulster within the Union; he had little concern for the rest of Ireland. He proved himself throughout to be an able defender of Ulster, and his organisational flair proved crucial to the success of the resistance campaign.

Both men had a powerful parliamentary ally in Andrew Bonar Law (1858–1923), leader of the Conservative Party since 1911. He was born in Canada and sat for a Scottish constituency but was of Presbyterian Ulster stock. Bonar Law's natural affinity for the unionist cause was given added pungency by his desire for British electoral advantage. Like Randolph Churchill before him, he seized upon home rule as a weapon with which to beat the government and quickly aligned himself with Carson's campaign. In July 1912 Bonar Law publicly denounced the Liberal alliance that led to Asquith's Home Rule Bill as a 'corrupt parliamentary bargain' with the Irish Parliamentary Party which would jeopardise the integrity of the empire. This was followed by the dark assertion that 'there are things stronger than parliamentary majorities' and a tacit incitement to civil war: 'I can imagine no length of resistance to which Ulster can go in which I should not be prepared to support them and in which they would not be supported by the majority of the British people.' For the democratic leader of the parliamentary party traditionally associated with law and order to sanction the use of extra-parliamentary force as a means of jettisoning government legislation was a truly extraordinary intervention which could only inflame sectarian passions further.

Bonar Law's rhetorical extremism was matched by Carson's orchestration of mass loyalist solidarity. On 28 September 1912 over 471,000 Ulster men and women signed the Solemn League and Covenant and the Declaration, in which they pledged to resist home rule 'using all means which may be found necessary'. But while the signatories were committing themselves to the maintenance of the unionist integrity of Ireland as a whole, Carson was formulating a tactical amendment to exclude all nine Ulster counties from the Bill. This was defeated in January 1913, however, and the Bill passed its third Commons reading.

The same month saw the formation of the paramilitary Ulster Volunteer Force by Carson and Craig, both of whom were eager to assert their political control over militant loyalists, who quickly joined up in their thousands. Ulstermen now began drilling in public, openly expressing their resolve to resist the implementation of home rule by force. The political implications seemed ominously clear: unionist leaders, no longer able to defeat home rule in parliament, were moving politics on to the streets, where deeds might achieve more than words.

Such a display of militant defiance, even if technically legal, represented a serious challenge to the government's authority in Ulster. Asquith's inaction, therefore, betrayed a fatal weakness which was seen by loyalists as vindicating their actions. The prime minister's hesitancy also encouraged Irish nationalists to imitate the unionists' example by forming the Irish Volunteers in Dublin in November 1913. The formation of such a paramilitary body posed a significant challenge to Redmond's leadership of nationalist Ireland, but for the time being he parried that threat by ensuring that many of his own nominees were appointed to the governing body of the Volunteers. There were now two private armies in Ireland, whose ability to mount a serious military threat was hampered only by their lack of sufficient arms.

This situation changed in April 1914 when German-purchased arms and ammunition were landed at three Ulster ports and quickly distributed to Ulster Volunteer Force members throughout the province, while the authorities stood by. This daring move was calculated to raise the political stakes, but in so doing the Ulster militants reintroduced the gun into Irish politics. Restless nationalists followed suit in July, when arms, again from Germany, were landed at Howth harbour near Dublin. Government forces intervened on this occasion, however, and four people were killed when troops fired on an unarmed crowd. Angry nationalists drew an invidious comparison between this prompt response and the authorities' inaction at the time of the Ulster gun-running.

Meanwhile, Asquith's Bill was progressing fitfully through the parliamentary process. It passed the Commons again in July 1913 only to be rejected again by the Lords. This was the last occasion on which the Lords could block the Bill, however; home rule now seemed destined to become law in 1914. This prospect concentrated the minds of the leading antagonists, many of whom, including Carson and Bonar Law, were privately resigned to some form of compromise based on the exclusion of all or part of Ulster. The idea of partition had earlier been mooted by a backbench Liberal MP, T.C. Agar-Robartes, but his proposal that the four most Protestant counties be excluded from the Bill was decisively rejected in June 1912. The idea was now revived by Lloyd George and then by Asquith, who tried to persuade Carson and Redmond to accept a partitionist compromise.

While the partition of Ireland proved attractive to British politicians in principle, it posed enormous problems in practice. The difficulty of establishing an equable, acceptable territorial division lay at the heart of the matter. Within Ulster, there were four overwhelmingly unionist counties (Antrim, Armagh, Down and Londonderry), three overwhelmingly nationalist counties (Donegal, Cavan and Monaghan) and two, Tyrone and Fermanagh, which were almost equally divided between the two parties. In the south, although unionism was a declining political force and Catholics were in the majority in most counties, there were areas – notably parts of Dublin and Wicklow – where Protestants predominated. It was inevitable, therefore, that a partitionist solution would leave large numbers of people on the wrong side of the border, wherever it was drawn. Asquith and Lloyd George persisted with the idea, however, and kept up the pressure on Carson and Redmond to agree to a settlement.

In March 1914 Redmond, still harbouring the illusion that Ulster was bluffing, eventually agreed to support Asquith's proposal to allow individual Ulster counties to opt out of home rule for a six-year period. The rationale behind this plan was that the Protestant parts of Ulster would, in the course of those six years, realise that they had nothing to fear from home rule, and so willingly accept integration thereafter. This was the maximum that Redmond was prepared to concede, but it was a dangerous concession. By accepting partition, however temporary, he was effectively accepting that Ireland was two nations, thereby flatly contradicting his assertion of October 1913 that 'Irish nationalists can never be assenting parties to the mutilation of the Irish nation. Ireland is a unit... The two-nation theory is to us an abomination and a blasphemy.' Carson, however, totally rejected the six-year time limit and told the Commons on 9 March 1914: 'Ulster wants this question settled now and for ever. We do not want a sentence of death with a stay of execution for six years.'

The unionists' rejection of a compromise based on

exclusion in March 1914 coincided with rumours that the Ulster Volunteer Force was planning to raid arms depots in Ulster. The government's decision that troops should be sent north to protect vulnerable depots alarmed many unionists, who interpreted the announcement as an attempt to coerce Ulster into accepting home rule. Amidst a confusion of military orders and fearing that they were being sent to disarm unionists, fifty-eight army officers at the Curragh military camp in County Kildare, led by General Hubert Gough, indicated that they would resign rather than lead their men against Ulster loyalists. The government, fearing a mutiny, summoned Gough to London, where he succeeded in extracting a written assurance from Colonel John Seely, secretary for war, that the army would not be used to impose home rule on Ulster. Although Asquith subsequently repudiated this concession and forced Seely to resign, the damage had already been done and a painful lesson learned: the government could not rely upon the army to enforce home rule in Ireland. The limits of official authority had again been exposed and the crisis deepened.

In an effort to prevent civil war, King George v convened an all-party conference at Buckingham Palace in July 1914. All the participants accepted the principle of partition; the problem lay in deciding the area of Ulster to be excluded and for how long. Agreement proved impossible, however, and the conference ended inconclusively after three days. Privately, Asquith expressed his exasperation at the now seemingly intractable nature of the Ulster question, angrily blaming 'that most damnable creation of the perverted ingenuity of man – the County of Tyrone' for its geographical obstinacy. Sadly, he would not be the last British politician whose failure to comprehend the intricacies of Irish political realities would end in impotent, imperial rage. Asquith, however, was luckier than many of his successors, in being rescued from the morass of Anglo-Irish politics by a greater European conflict, as the sudden outbreak of war in August 1914 swept Ireland's divisions up into a completely new political context.

10

REBELLION AND CIVIL WAR
1914–1923

The First World War, according to R.F. Foster, 'should be seen as one of the most decisive events in modern Irish history. Politically speaking, it temporarily defused the Ulster situation; it put home rule on ice; it altered the conditions of military crisis in Ireland at a stroke; and it created the rationale for an IRB rebellion.' The war also proved to be a defining moment for the political fortunes of John Redmond and the Irish Parliamentary Party. In a speech in the Commons on 3 August 1914, the day before Britain declared war on Germany, Redmond offered Asquith's government the support of nationalist Ireland, in the form of the Irish Volunteers, in the impending war effort. This gesture of Irish nationalist goodwill was calculated to impress British public and parliamentary opinion, and galvanise Asquith into placing the Home Rule Bill on the statute book. The tactic paid off when the Home Rule Act received the royal assent on

18 September, despite the walk-out of the entire Conservative opposition in the Commons. Irish self-government was now a legal, though not an actual, reality, as the implementation of the Act was suspended for the duration of the war. The position of Ulster remained ominously unresolved, however, as Westminster reserved the right to make as yet unspecified legislative arrangements for the province.

Buoyed up by this great political triumph, an invigorated Redmond, together with other nationalist and unionist parliamentarians, rallied Irish recruits to the British war effort. In an impromptu speech at Woodenbridge, County Wicklow, on 20 September he called on the Volunteers to join the British army and fight 'not only in Ireland itself, but wherever the firing line extends in defence of right, of freedom and of religion in this war'. These rousing words precipitated a dramatic crisis within the Volunteer movement, which led to a split between a majority who supported Redmond's recruitment policy and a minority, among them Eoin MacNeill, Patrick Pearse and Thomas MacDonagh, who opposed it. The former, possibly 180,000 strong, became known as the National Volunteers, while the dissenting 12,000 retained the title of Irish Volunteers.

Whereas constitutional Irish nationalists responded to Britain's war crisis with strategic but none the less heartfelt displays of patriotism, militant separatists demurred. In August 1914 the supreme council of the revitalised IRB decided that a nationwide rebellion should take place before the war ended. Guided by the ancient Fenian dictum that 'England's difficulty is Ireland's opportunity', the small inner circle of the IRB set about planning an insurrection. It was to be led by the Irish Volunteers, supported by Clan na Gael funds from America and German arms. In December 1915 the IRB military council, comprising Pearse, Tom Clarke, Seán Mac Diarmada, Éamon

Ceannt and Joseph Plunkett, secretly decided upon Easter Sunday, 23 April 1916, as the date for the rising. It was these five revolutionaries, together with labour leader James Connolly, commander of the socialist Irish Citizen Army, and Thomas MacDonagh, poet and lecturer, who planned the insurrection.

Rumours of an intended rising reached Dublin Castle in March and early April, yet the authorities had no definite proof of a rebellious plot until Easter Saturday, when they received news of the arrest of Sir Roger Casement in Kerry on Good Friday. Casement, a retired Dublin-born colonial civil servant, had been landed by a German submarine a few hours earlier, having spent the previous months in Germany trying to secure government support for the planned rising and recruit Irish prisoners of war for the IRB. Even after his arrest, the authorities took no immediate action, on the assumption that this setback had scuppered the rebels' plans. The *Aud*, a German ship laden with arms, was scuttled by its captain in Queenstown (now Cobh) harbour in Cork, having failed to rendezvous as planned with Casement.

On Easter Saturday the Volunteer commander, Eoin MacNeill, on realising that he had been duped by Pearse and Plunkett into sanctioning special Volunteer manoeuvres, issued an order countermanding all military action. This had the effect of confusing the Volunteers and preventing a nationwide insurrection. It also postponed the start of the rising by one day.

So when, at noon on Easter Monday, Pearse proclaimed the establishment of an Irish republic from the steps of the General Post Office in Dublin, he knew that military failure was almost inevitable. But Ireland's honour might still be saved by a blood sacrifice, since 'from the graves of patriot men and women spring living nations'. Pearse's words are a reminder that the rising was the product of a specifically Catholic political consciousness – it did, after all, coincide with Easter, the festival which commemorates Christ's resurrection – and as such remains a potent historical testament to the intimate link between religion and nationalism in Ireland. Yet it was the Protestant Yeats who, in seeing in the events of Easter week the birth of a 'terrible beauty', brilliantly encapsulated the conflicting mixture of pity, horror and admiration which the insurgents' deeds evoked in the minds of many Irish nationalists, then and since.

Lacking widespread popular support, the rebellion was crushed within days and Pearse surrendered unconditionally on Saturday 29 April. He and the other commanders of the rising were imprisoned in Kilmainham jail, where they were hastily tried in secret by court martial and sentenced to death. The decision to execute the rebel leaders was politically disastrous from a British government perspective, as it created martyrs for the republican cause and greatly alienated Irish public opinion at home and abroad, especially in America. The first of the executions took place on 3 May when Pearse, MacDonagh and Clarke were shot. Twelve more executions followed over the next nine days, despite veteran nationalist MP John Dillon's Commons' warning that the government was 'washing out our whole life work in a sea of blood'. Although Asquith halted the killings after 12 May, Irish political opinion was already beginning to desert constitutional nationalism. Whereas few Irish people, nationalist or otherwise, had supported the rebels during Easter week, the tide of political opinion now turned in their favour. As with many Irish revolutionaries before them, their failure – and their cause – had been ennobled by their deaths.

Unlike 1798 and 1867, however, the ferocity of the government's response in 1916 legitimised the violence of the revolutionaries in the minds of a great many Irish people, who were no longer prepared to trust the British government to deliver them into a self-governing Ireland. Nor were they willing to support those Irish politicians who continued to put their faith in 'perfidious Albion'. This had serious implications for Redmond and his party, whose policy of winning home rule by constitutional means was dealt a devastating blow by the rising. In the months that followed, a decisive transformation began to take shape in Irish politics, as public support shifted from the discredited constitutional nationalism of the Irish Parliamentary Party to the militant republicanism of Sinn Féin, an amalgam of different groups which was coming increasingly under the direction of republicans. Although Sinn Féin played no direct part in the rising, the authorities subsequently labelled it the Sinn Féin rebellion, thereby giving the moribund movement and its members an unearned nationalist prestige.

Another key factor which alienated Irish nationalist opinion and encouraged Sinn Féin support was the threat of military conscription. As the flow of volunteers to the British army began to dry up, conscription was enforced in Britain in 1916, but even before the rising, it was judged prudent not to attempt to include Ireland. British ministers nevertheless returned repeatedly to the theme of Irish conscription during the latter part of the war. After the defeat of Russia in March 1918, the Germans launched a new offensive on the western front, thereby increasing Britain's recruitment needs. The cabinet decided to increase conscription in Britain, but could not do so unless they also tapped the reservoir of military potential in Ireland.

Thus, in April 1918 Lloyd George, by then prime minister, introduced a Bill to extend conscription to Ireland, linking it with a revived promise of implementing home rule. He did so despite warnings from John Dillon (1851–1927), the newly elected leader of the Irish party following Redmond's death in March, who withdrew his MPs from the Commons in protest.

The whole of nationalist Ireland – home rulers, Sinn Féiners, the trade unions, the Catholic hierarchy – condemned the proposal and united in a massive demonstration of solidarity against this imposition. In the event, the failure of the German offensive in June 1918 reduced the need for extra men and the Military Service Act was never applied to Ireland. Yet the crisis had a great effect on Irish politics. It forced the Irish Parliamentary Party to adopt the Sinn Féin tactic of absenting themselves from Westminster and in so doing discredited their previous policy. Lloyd George's short-sighted measure thus diminished the standing of the Irish nationalist parliamentarians, which it was in his government's interest to support, while vindicating the absentionist arguments of Sinn Féin.

With the national mood of resentment provoked by Britain's inept handling of the rising heightened by continuing martial law and the threat of conscription, Sinn Féin sought to translate this new-found prestige into electoral support, under its new leader Eamon de Valera (1882–1975), the senior surviving commander of the rising. During 1917 the party made considerable advances, winning by-elections in North Roscommon in February and South Longford in May, constituencies previously held by home rulers. In July a key by-election took place in East Clare, caused by the death in action on the western front of Major William Redmond, younger brother of John. It was Daniel O'Connell's by-election victory in the same county in 1828 which had set in motion the chain of events leading to Catholic emancipation in 1829. Almost a century later, the county was again the locus of decisive political change. De Valera contested the seat and during the campaign made clear that he wanted a sovereign, independent Irish republic. His sweeping victory meant that the majority of the electors had decisively rejected the Irish Parliamentary Party and had opted for the republican ideals proclaimed in 1916.

Almost immediately after the armistice of 11 November 1918, Lloyd George called a general election with the wartime coalition government still extant. The British and Irish electorate, which had been greatly increased as a result of the Representation of the People Act earlier that year, included virtually all men and, for the first time, many women. In Britain, the government won a huge majority, but Conservative supporters of the coalition were much more numerous than Liberals. In Ireland, Sinn Féin won a spectacular victory, taking 73 of Ireland's 105 seats and reducing home rule representation to a mere 6. This outcome showed that home rule was now a tarnished, even outdated concept, which paled beside the bright prospect of an Irish republic. The Irish Parliamentary Party's obsolescence was further underlined by the youthful dynamism of the Sinn Féin leadership, whose republican ideology caught the imagination of many of Ireland's newly enfranchised voters.

Having declared that its elected members would refuse to attend Westminster, Sinn Féin MPs met instead in the Mansion House in Dublin on 21 January 1919. They declared a sovereign Irish Republic and established a parliament, Dáil Éireann, to legislate for all Ireland, hoping that the new state would be granted self-determination at the Paris Peace Conference. This illegal act was, of course, highly provocative in that it constituted the establishment of a rival government to the British administration based in Dublin Castle, and as such could not go unchallenged by the authorities. Yet despite the strenuous efforts of the British, and the fact that many deputies were in prison, the Dáil did manage to operate an alternative system of government by creating ministries, setting up courts and collecting taxes. This executive challenge to the British administration had a military counterpart, as on the very same day as the Dáil was established, two members of the Royal Irish

Constabulary were ambushed and killed at Soloheadbeg in County Tipperary by an Irish Volunteer unit. This incident marked the start of the Anglo-Irish War, also known as the War of Independence, which was to last until July 1921.

Refusing to negotiate a political settlement, Lloyd George's government sought to pacify Ireland by repressive military means. Throughout the war, the authorities refused to concede publicly that its opponents, the republican Volunteers or, as they came to be known, the Irish Republican Army, constituted a proper army. Instead, Lloyd George continually referred to it as 'a murder gang' to be dealt with by the police, supported by the army, and not vice versa. (A similar approach underpinned Britain's 'criminalisation' and 'Ulsterisation' policies in Northern Ireland in the 1970s.) So although troops were used to counter IRA violence, a campaign was launched to find British recruits for the Royal Irish Constabulary, as young Irishmen were not joining. Two additional police units, the Black and Tans – nicknamed partly after the hounds of a famous hunt and partly because they wore army khaki trousers and dark green police tunics – and the Auxiliaries were hastily recruited from the ranks of the one million demobilised British servicemen. These new recruits, the first of which arrived in Ireland in March 1920, were greatly lacking in police discipline and soon earned a gruesome reputation. Consequently, their undisciplined acts of brutality and terror against the Irish civilian population entered deeply into the Irish nationalist consciousness and engendered widespread sympathy and support for the IRA.

Directed by Michael Collins (1890–1922), who also held the post of finance minister in the underground government of the putative republic, the IRA evolved into an effective guerrilla army in the course of the two-and-a-half-year war. Its members specialised in sporadic attacks and assassinations upon British military installations and personnel, often carried out by well-trained, highly mobile armed units called 'flying columns', which struck at the enemy with devastating efficiency. Collins's avowed aim was to make Ireland effectively ungovernable and thereby force the British government to concede independence. Cold-blooded killings were carried out by both crown and republican forces, as a ruthless pattern of assassination and reprisal took shape, culminating in the events of Bloody Sunday, 21 November 1920. That morning, the IRA killed fourteen British officers in Dublin on suspicion of their being secret government agents. Later that day in the city, the Black and Tans opened fire at a GAA football match in Croke Park, causing twelve deaths and injuring many more.

In the autumn of 1919 Lloyd George's coalition government turned again to consider the Irish question. The recommendation of a special cabinet committee that not one but two home rule parliaments be established in Ireland was now adopted as government policy. This was embodied in the Government of Ireland Act passed in December 1920 and effective from 1 May 1921. The Act partitioned Ireland into two jurisdictions, 'Northern Ireland', defined as 'the six parliamentary counties of Antrim, Armagh, Down, Fermanagh, Londonderry and Tyrone, and the parliamentary boroughs of Belfast and Londonderry', and 'Southern Ireland', comprising the remaining twenty-six counties. This Act, the most momentous piece of British legislation to affect Ireland in 120 years, was a compromise solution which failed to satisfy any of the competing strands of Irish political opinion. It was, in effect, a British solution to an Irish problem.

In May 1921 elections were held under the terms of the Act in both parts of Ireland. Northern unionists' initial reluctance to accept the settlement and relinquish the goal of full integration with the United Kingdom soon gave way to a pragmatic

resolve to secure comprehensive parliamentary control by returning forty unionist MPs to the fifty-two-seat assembly. The
Act proved largely inoperative in the south, however, where
Sinn Féin leaders rejected its legitimacy and instead used the
election to renew their mandate by returning 124 members –
known as TDs (Teachta Dála) – to the second Dáil, which convened on 16 August 1921.

By then, however, neither side in the conflict could see any
immediate prospect of military victory. The IRA was tiring and
the government's military strategy in Ireland, particularly the
policy of reprisals, was causing increasing criticism in Britain
and abroad. Contacts between government officials and Sinn
Féin representatives led to a truce being brokered, which came
into effect on 11 July. The following day, de Valera, as president of Dáil Éireann, led a delegation to London to meet
Lloyd George for preliminary discussions. A state of deadlock
quickly emerged, however, as de Valera insisted upon an independent all-Ireland republic, whereas Lloyd George was only
willing to concede limited dominion status for the twenty-six
counties. Much correspondence between the two men followed during the next two months, as they sought to find a
compromise solution and so move beyond the precarious truce
to a final negotiated settlement. The prime minister finally invited de Valera to send delegates to a London conference
which opened on 11 October to determine 'how the association of Ireland with the community of nations known as the
British Empire may best be reconciled with Irish national
aspirations'.

At the outset, reconciliation seemed an impossibility, given
the diametrically opposed demands of the two sides. For the
Irish delegation, led by Griffith and Collins, independence
and unity were the most important issues. A republic had been
proclaimed and died for; it would not be easily relinquished.

Significantly, de Valera himself did not go to London, knowing, perhaps, that some sort of compromise on the ideal of a republic was inevitable. The twin British priorities were the obverse of the Irish ones; the retention of Ireland within the empire and the maintenance of partition, given that the Northern Ireland state had already been established. The Ulster unionists, moreover, had made it abundantly clear that they were prepared to go to any lengths to maintain the Union and resist rule by Dublin.

Negotiations dragged on for several weeks. The issue of the permanent partition of Ireland, which was wholly unacceptable to the republican delegates, was skilfully sidelined by Lloyd George by means of a proposal to establish an intergovernmental commission to review the existing border at a future date. Discussions focused instead on Ireland's constitutional status within the empire, eventually centring on a semantic dispute over the wording of an oath of allegiance to the British monarch. Finally, after eight weeks of tortuous negotiations, Lloyd George, seizing upon divisions within the Irish team, presented them with an urgent ultimatum: agree to a settlement or face 'war within three days'. Partial Irish sovereignty was available, but not the hallowed republic. His ploy worked, and the six Irish delegates signed the Anglo-Irish Treaty in Downing Street at 2.10 a.m. on 6 December 1921. It was, all knew, a fateful hour, none more so perhaps than Collins, who in signing the treaty predicted that he was signing his own death warrant.

The treaty conferred dominion status on the Irish Free State, the new name for the twenty-six counties, which would remain within the British Empire. All members of the Dublin parliament would have to swear an oath of allegiance to the British monarch who would be represented in Ireland by a governor-general. The Free State would have full governmental control over its internal affairs, including the judiciary, police and a limited army, though Britain retained control of certain strategic ports. On the crucial issue of partition, the right of Northern Ireland to opt out from the provisions of the treaty, and so remain part of the United Kingdom, was enshrined in Article 12. If this were to happen, an inter-governmental body known as the Boundary Commission would be appointed to 'determine in accordance with the wishes of the inhabitants, so far as may be compatible with economic and geographic conditions, the boundaries between Northern Ireland and the rest of Ireland'.

The treaty pleased none of the contending sides in full. Although it was welcomed by many in Britain as the final solution to the long-running Irish question, this was not so. Not only had northern unionists been given that which they did not want – a home rule parliament in Belfast – they had also abandoned their southern counterparts, who now constituted a small minority in the Free State. Northern nationalists were equally unhappy about their abandonment by pro-treaty Sinn Féin in a state with a built-in unionist majority. Unlike southern unionists, however, they made up a substantial minority of the Northern Ireland population and, as will be seen, never became fully reconciled to the new state. In Britain, the agreement proved similarly divisive. Many Liberals blamed Lloyd George, not so much for the treaty itself, but for the government's conduct of the Anglo-Irish War. As for the Liberals' Conservative associates in the coalition, the agreement seriously undermined their claim to be the party of the Union, since the government of which they were part had now conceded to most of Ireland a greater degree of self-government than O'Connell or Parnell had demanded. But it was among the nationalists of the south that the bitterness was greatest, the agony most poignant.

The treaty caused deep divisions within the republican cabinet, the Dáil and the country at large. Sovereignty rather than unity – the oath rather than partition – emerged as *the* divisive issue. Pragmatists like Collins defended the agreement as the best available compromise and a stepping stone to full independence, saying that it 'gives us freedom, not the ultimate freedom that all nations desire and develop to, but the freedom to achieve it'. The republican idealists who opposed the treaty, led by de Valera, criticised it for failing to deliver the hoped-for republic, and condemned it as being 'in violent conflict with the wishes of the majority of this nation'.

The protracted and acrimonious Dáil debate which ensued culminated in the narrow ratification of the treaty by 64 votes to 57 on 7 January 1922. De Valera promptly resigned as president of the Dáil and led the anti-treatyites out of the chamber, while the remaining members proceeded to establish a provisional government under the terms of the agreement. This body was set up to facilitate the transfer of power from Britain and the subsequent transition to full government, which, under the terms of the treaty, was due to take effect from 6 December 1922, exactly one year after the agreement was signed. On 16 January 1922 Collins, as chairman of this new body, went to Dublin Castle where a formal transfer of power from the British to the Irish authorities took place. He had, in effect, become the first leader of independent Ireland.

Tension between pro- and anti-treaty forces mounted in the months that followed, as British forces evacuated army barracks throughout the country and the RIC was replaced by an unarmed Irish police force. The IRA split, with the pro-treaty faction forming the new Free State army. A blatant challenge to the authority of the provisional government came in April when anti-treaty republicans occupied the Four Courts in Dublin, the centre of the Irish judiciary, and established their military headquarters there. Reluctant to move against his old comrades and precipitate open conflict, Collins played for time. Meanwhile, the Irish general election in June showed that a clear majority of the electorate was in favour of the 1921 agreement. Fifty-eight pro-treaty candidates were returned, as against 36 anti-treatyites, with the remaining 34 seats divided between the Labour Party and other groups.

Hopes of peaceful reconciliation between pro- and anti-treatyites were short-lived, however. Two acts of republican defiance – the assassination of Sir Henry Wilson, military adviser to the new Northern Ireland government, by republican sympathisers in London on 22 June, followed by the kidnapping of a leading Free State army commander in Dublin four days later – meant that decisive government action could no longer be postponed. In the early hours of 28 June 1922 the provisional government issued an ultimatum to the republican garrison in the Four Courts to surrender immediately. When the order was ignored, pro-treaty troops began to shell the building with guns and ammunition supplied by the departing British. The Irish Civil War had begun.

The ten months of bloody, brutal fighting that followed divided families and communities, as men who had recently been comrades against a common enemy now turned their guns on each other. Most of the fighting took place in the countryside, especially in the Munster counties of Tipperary, Cork, Kerry and Limerick, and involved guerrilla ambushes and reprisals. As the war progressed, the provisional government dealt with republican forces, now known as Irregulars, with growing ruthlessness. Between November 1922 and May 1923 the government summarily executed seventy-seven anti-treatyite prisoners in response to republican attacks on TDs and senators, members of the upper house of the new Irish legislature.

The war robbed the nation of some of its finest leaders, including Cathal Brugha, Arthur Griffith, Liam Mellows and, aged only thirty-one, Michael Collins, killed in an ambush in his native Cork in August 1922. He was succeeded as chairman of the provisional government by William T. Cosgrave (1880–1965) in September. Three months later, in the midst of the internecine chaos and to some extent eclipsed by it, the Irish Free State (Saorstát Éireann) formally came into existence, one year after the signing of the treaty. By the time the republicans were ground into submission by the numerically superior and better-equipped government forces in May 1923, as many as four thousand lives had been lost and countless others traumatised by their experiences. Considerable damage had also been done to the country's infrastructure, trade and industry, leaving the fledgling state with a crippling financial burden.

The Civil War represented the worst possible start for the new southern state. Instead of looking forward to the creation of a new society, Irish people were compelled to endure the fierce embrace of the past. The war left a legacy of great bitterness, traces of which are still discernible in Irish life today. The treaty became the central political issue in independent Ireland and the divisions it produced formed the basis for the Irish party system. The two main parties that subsequently came to dominate politics – Fianna Fáil (a Sinn Féin progeny) and Fine Gael (successor to Cosgrave's renamed pro-treaty party, Cumann na nGaedheal) – originated in the divided loyalties of the early 1920s and cast a long shadow over the emergence of other political ideologies. In particular, the struggle for independence arrested the development of embryonic socialist and feminist movements in Ireland, leading to the marginalisation of female and working-class voices in the political life of the new state. This polarisation of Irish politics around attitudes to the national question meant that the country evolved a different political culture from many other European countries, where social and economic divisions often provide the basis for political representation. Over seventy years later, it is these same two parties that continue to dominate the political scene, despite the rising profile of the Labour Party. In the north, too, the national question continued to dominate politics and inhibit the development of a political culture based on people's social and economic needs.

11

FROM FREE STATE TO REPUBLIC
1923–1959

In May 1923 the Civil War formally ended. Three months later, the first general election under the new Irish Free State constitution took place. This election, like all held in the south since, was based on the system of proportional representation, which effectively guarantees that the results are a fair reflection of the voters' wishes. The electorate entrusted the formidable task of building a state from the rubble of revolution to Cumann na nGaedheal, which won 63 of the 153 seats. Anti-treatyite Sinn Féin won 44 seats, with the remainder being shared almost equally between the Labour Party, the Farmers' Party and independents.

As in many post-revolutionary societies, the intractability of inherited realities dictated that tradition rather than experiment characterised the policies and practice of the new government. The Cosgrave administration was naturally conservative in character and showed a notable degree of continuity with the

ancien régime, so much so that Ronan Fanning has observed that
the new state was marked, 'not by a commitment to cast off
British influence, but by an extraordinary fidelity to British
models'. And if Cumann na nGaedheal was naturally conservative, it was difficult to discern much sign of radicalism in the
government's political opponents.

While the army and police force were fundamentally re-
structured, the political institutions, civil service and legal and
educational systems did not change radically after independence. The government's systematic attempt to revive the Irish
language, which led to the promotion of Gaelic as the language
of instruction in most primary schools and a prerequisite for
employment in certain state posts, represented a rare, and ultimately futile, attempt to translate revolutionary idealism into
post-revolutionary reality. The boast of one of the leading
ministers of the new state was justified: the first generation of
Irish self-governors showed themselves to be the most conservative of revolutionaries.

The conservative tendencies of Cosgrave and his colleagues were deepened by their overriding need to legitimise
and consolidate their authority throughout the twenty-six-
county state. While the abstentionism of de Valera's Sinn
Féin strengthened the government's parliamentary authority, the defeated republican forces posed a serious extra-
parliamentary threat to the legitimacy of the new regime, as
the assassination of the vice-president and minister for justice,
Kevin O'Higgins, in July 1927 graphically demonstrated.
Fearful of a return to the anarchy of civil war, the government
courted the support of those sectors of society with vested
interests in the maintenance of political and economic stability:
businessmen, prosperous farmers and an increasingly influential Catholic hierarchy.

The result was a polity characterised by fiscal prudence

and social conservatism. Economic policy was based on a commitment to develop the dominant agricultural sector at the expense of the weak industrial sector. Episcopal concerns about public morality led to laws being passed to protect the nation's purity from such perceived moral contaminants as films, novels, contraceptives and divorce. The common concern of Church and state to build a nation upon Catholic nationalist principles led to the passing of a draconian Censorship of Publications Act in 1929. This Act was used to ban not only genuine pornography, but also serious work by many Irish writers, including James Joyce, Sean O'Casey and Frank O'Connor, whose realistic perspectives were considered a threat to the national self-image of moral and cultural purity. Such measures helped create an authoritarian and censorious social climate which inhibited cultural expression and confirmed Ulster Protestants' perception that the largely homogeneous Catholic south was becoming a strongly confessional state, thereby hardening the partitionist divide.

The reality of partition was formally consolidated in 1925 following the deliberations of the Boundary Commission, which was established under the treaty to readjust the border between Northern Ireland and the Free State. Negotiations ended ignominiously for the southern government when Cosgrave signed a tripartite agreement with British Prime Minister Stanley Baldwin (1867–1947) and Northern Ireland premier James Craig to accept the territorial status quo, thereby effectively ending Dublin dreams of reunification. In reality, the Irish government, having just experienced a bloody civil war over the treaty, had no real enthusiasm for reviving the whole border issue and exacerbating existing divisions within the Free State. Nor did the British government wish to reopen the old wounds of Ireland and its internal boundaries. The outcome represented a major victory for Craig, however, and a painful realisation by northern Catholics that they would have to accept the reality of their position in the Northern Ireland state. Meanwhile in the south, the Boundary Commission débâcle deepened the conviction of militant republicans that partition could be removed only by physical force, while strengthening the resolve of de Valera and his followers to abandon abstentionism and enter the constitutional arena.

Thus, in May 1926 de Valera launched a new republican party, Fianna Fáil, dedicated to the establishment of an independent, self-sufficient, Irish-speaking united Ireland by constitutional means. Within a year, the party had dramatically supplanted Sinn Féin as the popular voice of Irish republicanism. Fianna Fáil won forty-four seats in the 1927 general election, after which de Valera took the crucial decision to lead his deputies into the Dáil, formally taking the odious oath of allegiance to the British monarch, while informally denying he was doing so. The party's transition from parliamentary opposition to government occurred five years later in 1932, when de Valera succeeded Cosgrave as premier of the Irish Free State and began sixteen years of uninterrupted Fianna Fáil rule.

De Valera's primary political objective was to expunge all references to the British crown from the Irish constitution in order to bring about his cherished goal of full Irish sovereignty. He was assisted considerably in this objective by a piece of British legislation, the 1931 Statute of Westminster, which (without explicitly saying so, but by necessary implication) acknowledged the right of any dominion to secede from the Commonwealth. Within months of coming to power he initiated war with Britain on two fronts, constitutional and economic. His constitutional crusade began with the abolition of the oath of allegiance and the downgrading of the office of governor-general. In 1936 he took advantage of the abdication of King Edward VIII to remove the crown from the existing constitution as far as internal Irish affairs were concerned. The accompanying External Relations Act empowered the king to act on behalf of the Free State in certain external matters, on the advice of the Irish government. Such opportunism brought closer de Valera's proclaimed goal of full sovereignty and cleared the way for the publication of a new constitution on 1 May 1937, which was ratified by the Dáil in June and passed by referendum on 1 July.

The new constitution came into operation on 29 December 1937 and remains the fundamental law of the state. It made Éire, the new name for the Free State, a de facto republic, with a president, an elected figurehead with limited political powers, as head of state and a prime minister or *taoiseach* as head of government. De Valera stopped short of formally proclaiming a republic on the grounds that the nation was not yet unified. Nevertheless, Articles 2 and 3 asserted the Dublin government's constitutional right to exercise jurisdiction over the six northern counties, a claim which was the target of much unionist resentment until its proposed removal by referendum in May 1998.

One article which attracted little criticism at the time but subsequently led to widespread disquiet is that which refers to the position of women in Ireland. Article 41 enshrines the idea that a woman's natural and proper place is in the home as a full-time wife and mother. It reflects the patriarchal consensus that underpinned official attitudes to women in post-independence Ireland, a consensus which enabled successive governments to enact a series of discriminatory laws curtailing women's political, economic and reproductive rights. The fact that no woman contributed to the drafting of the constitution further illustrates this female marginalisation. It was not until the 1970s, with Ireland's entry into Europe and the emergence of a vibrant Irish feminist movement, that many of the discriminatory laws against women began to be changed and the patriarchal bias redressed. Ireland's first female minister, since 1922, Máire Geoghegan-Quinn, was appointed minister for the Gaeltacht in 1979 and eleven years later the Republic elected its first woman president, Mary Robinson, whose victory was widely seen as a symbolic milestone in Irish women's painful journey towards full and equal citizenship.

On the economic front, from July 1932 de Valera withheld land annuity payments due to Britain under the Land Acts of the late nineteenth and early twentieth centuries. When Britain retaliated by imposing tariffs on Irish produce entering the United Kingdom, the so-called Anglo-Irish 'economic war' began. Hostilities lasted for almost six years, during which time the Irish economy generally, and the farming community in particular, suffered great hardship. The first move to resolve the impasse came in November 1937, when de Valera raised the prospect of a negotiated settlement with Neville Chamberlain, the new British prime minister. Talks began in London in January 1938 and ended successfully with the signing of the Anglo-Irish Agreement on 25 April, whereby the Irish government agreed to a one-off payment of £10 million to settle the land annuities dispute, and duty-free trade between the two countries resumed.

These years also witnessed a fundamental economic shift away from free trade towards a policy of industrial protectionism, the corollary of de Valera's vision of frugal self-sufficiency and pastoral isolation, which he so eloquently evoked in his celebrated Saint Patrick's Day radio broadcast of 1943:

The Ireland which we have dreamed of would be the home of a people who valued material wealth only as a basis of right living, of a people who were satisfied with frugal comfort and devoted their leisure to things of the spirit; a land whose countryside would be bright with cosy homesteads, whose fields and villages would be joyous with the sounds of industry, with the romping of sturdy children, the contests of athletic youths, the laughter of comely maidens; whose firesides would be forums for the wisdom of serene old age. It would, in a word, be the home of a people living the life that God desires that men should live.

This sonorous vision encapsulated de Valera's conception of Ireland as a Gaelic, Catholic utopia in an unprincipled, materialistic world. It was a dream that bore little relationship to Irish reality, however, as the high levels of poverty, unemployment and emigration which characterised his premiership attest.

The Anglo-Irish Agreement of 1938 which brought the trade war to an end also provided for the return to the state of the three ports (Berehaven, Cobh and Lough Swilly) retained by the British under the treaty, thus making Irish sovereignty a twenty-six-county reality. The first exercise in national sovereignty occurred in September 1939 when de Valera proclaimed Ireland's neutrality on the outbreak of the Second World War or, as it was known in Ireland, 'the Emergency'. This declaration represented a clear determination to pursue an independent foreign policy in international relations and received overwhelming support from all parties in the Dáil. In fact, so great was all-party support for the government's non-aligned stance that a leading member of the main opposition party, Fine Gael (constituted from Cumann na nGaedheal and some smaller groups in 1933), was actually expelled from his party for expressing a different view in 1942. While partition was the ostensible reason for Irish neutrality, non-participation in the war was also desirable from the point of view of internal state security – there were fears that an IRA–Nazi pact might destabilise the state – and the economy. But whereas the proclamation of neutrality was a straightforward affair, its preservation required considerable diplomatic skill.

De Valera demonstrated adroit statecraft in maintaining Ireland's formal non-alignment, not least in his rejection of Prime Minister Churchill's seductive offers of Irish unity in return for Allied alignment. As the conflict went on, however, the government's officially neutral stance was belied by its covert support for the Allied war effort, which involved the sharing of Irish air space and intelligence information with Britain, and a passive acquiescence in the steady stream of Irish recruits to the British forces. Yet Ireland's policy of friendly neutrality did not prevent Churchill from launching an imperious attack on de Valera's isolationism in his victory broadcast of May 1945, an attack prompted by the latter's formal expression of condolences to the German people on the death of Hitler. Unwise though the taoiseach's gesture was, he soon recovered his poise by issuing a restrained and dignified response to Churchill's broadside.

The immediate post-war years were characterised by socio-economic gloom brought about by continuing shortages of food and fuel, rising prices, increasing unemployment (despite high emigration) and a series of poor harvests. A Fianna Fáil administration, jaded after sixteen years in power, bore the brunt of popular dissatisfaction in the 1948 general election and was replaced by a five-party coalition government under the premiership of Fine Gael's John A. Costello (1891–1976). The impact of this new government on Anglo-Irish relations was immediate and dramatic. On 7 September 1948, during an official visit to Canada, Costello announced his government's intention to declare Ireland a republic and secede from the Commonwealth. This involved revoking the 1936 External Relations Act, which authorised the king to act in the appointment of Irish diplomatic representatives on the advice of the Irish government. The announcement surprised many people, as Fine Gael was generally regarded as the more pro-British party. Repeal legislation was passed by the Dáil in December and the formal inauguration of the Republic of Ireland followed on Easter Monday 1949, the thirty-third anniversary of the 1916 rising. Thus, Costello completed the process of dismantling the treaty which de Valera had initiated in 1932, thereby fulfilling the latter's proclaimed strategy of April 1933: 'Let us remove these forms one by one, so that this state we control may become a republic in fact; and that, when the time comes, the proclaiming of the republic may involve no more than a ceremony, the formal confirmation of a status already attained.'

Not surprisingly, these precipitous constitutional man-oeuvres provoked alarm among northern unionists, who viewed them as yet another putative threat to partition. Re-newed fears of a recrudescent southern irredentism prompted Prime Minister Basil Brooke (1888–1973) to extract guarantees from Clement Attlee's Labour government that Northern Ireland's constitutional position within the United Kingdom would be safeguarded. The resultant Ireland Act of June 1949 affirmed that 'in no event will Northern Ireland or any part thereof cease to be part of His Majesty's dominions and of the United Kingdom without the consent of the parlia-ment of Northern Ireland'. This retaliatory Act disabused southern anti-partitionists of their lingering unificatory notions and proved yet again, in the words of Fanning, that 'the achievement of sovereignty took precedence over the aspiration to unity in the minds of those who controlled the destiny of independent Ireland'.

The 1950s were a time of prolonged economic stagnation in Ireland. At a time when other European countries were undergoing post-war modernising developments and implementing socio-economic reforms, the Republic remained stuck in an isolationist and protectionist mode. Unemployment reached a record seventy-eight thousand in 1957, pushing the already soaring emigration rate even higher. Over four hundred thousand people left Ireland in the decade from 1951 to 1961, the greatest exodus since the 1880s, which brought the population down to a mere 2.8 million. The reasons for emigration were not solely economic; the stifling cultural and intellectual climate drove many to seek more propitious life opportunities elsewhere.

Whereas nineteenth-century Irish migration was mainly to America, the vast majority of mid-twentieth-century Irish emigrants settled in Britain, where they played a major role in the post-war rebuilding programme. The 1948 British Nationality Act recognised the 'special position' of citizens of the Irish Republic, and Britain continued to treat Irish immigrants as Commonwealth citizens even after the 1949 Ireland Act. Many of de Valera's mythic cosy homesteads became all too real ruined cottages during these years, deserted by thousands of mostly rural Irish men and women. Meanwhile, politicians dithered, unable or unwilling to stop this national haemorrhage, some even regarding emigration as an inevitable and not altogether unwelcome social fact.

Costello's ideologically disparate coalition finally crumbled in the spring of 1951 in the aftermath of a controversy over the introduction of a state medical service for mothers and children by the socialist minister for health, Dr Noel Browne. His 'mother-and-child' scheme, which proposed to offer free healthcare to mothers and children under sixteen, was successfully opposed by Catholic churchmen, thereby revealing the extent to which ministerial freedom continued to be circumscribed by episcopal influence. From a northern perspective, the controversy further reinforced Protestants' view of the south as a Catholic theocracy. Fianna Fáil was returned to power in the resultant election but only as a weak, minority government, which gave way to a second Costello-led coalition in 1954.

Three years later the redoubtable de Valera, now seventy-five and almost blind, was elected taoiseach for the final time, as Fianna Fáil began another unbroken sixteen years in office. When, in June 1959, this colossus of modern Irish politics finally resigned the leadership of his party to become the country's third president, the state he had so profoundly shaped was ready to embrace social, economic and cultural changes so far-reaching as to render his cherished myth of a pastoral, Gaelic Ireland finally and utterly obsolete.

12
UNIONISM AND NATIONALISM IN NORTHERN IRELAND
1920–1968

The Northern Ireland state came into existence as a result of the Government of Ireland Act which finally passed through the Westminster parliament on 23 December 1920 and took effect in May 1921. This Act, as has been seen, provided for the setting up of two governments and two parliaments in Ireland, one for the six counties which were to form Northern Ireland, the other for the remaining twenty-six counties in southern Ireland. Each of these parliaments would be concerned exclusively with government of its own part of Ireland, while matters which concerned the United Kingdom as a whole would continue to be decided at Westminster, and MPs from both parts of Ireland would continue to sit there. The UK parliament was to retain the power to override the Irish parliaments, a measure which was to prove very important many years later.

In the south the Act was virtually a dead letter as Sinn Féin refused to recognise it. Northern unionists had not wanted such an arrangement and only came to accept it as 'a supreme sacrifice'. They would have preferred to remain directly under the United Kingdom parliament but, as Charles Craig, brother of James, the first prime minister of Northern Ireland, told the Commons in 1920: 'We believe that so long as we were without a Parliament of our own constant attacks would be made upon us, and constant attempts would be made . . . to draw us into a Dublin Parliament. We see our safety, therefore, in having a Parliament of our own.'

Many British and southern Irish politicians viewed the partition settlement as a temporary measure, envisaging an eventual reconciliation between north and south. The 1920 Act reflected this by proposing to set up a Council of Ireland, consisting of northern and southern representatives, to facilitate the process. This notion of an all-Ireland dimension to north–south relations was to remain a feature of subsequent British governments' attempts to resolve the Irish question up to the present day. However, the concept of a unitary state was anathema to northern Protestants, who continued to fear that their religious interests and economic well-being would be jeopardised in any all-Ireland parliament dominated by a Catholic majority.

Northern unionists quickly came to appreciate the merits of having their own state as a protection against enemies both within and without. These enemies were the Catholic minority in the north, many of whom refused to accept the legitimacy of the Northern Ireland state, and the various southern political parties and groups, including the IRA, who wished to achieve a united Ireland. British politicians themselves could not be fully trusted, as northern unionists feared that at some time in the future a Westminster government might be tempted for its own reasons to negotiate a deal with the south, by which unionist interests would be overridden, and they would be forced into the southern state.

Having reluctantly accepted a parliament of their own, the unionists were able to force a major concession from the British government regarding the area of the new state. This was not to be the nine counties of the historical province of Ulster, but rather the six north-eastern counties, which meant that the overall Protestant majority in the new state was 65 per cent, whereas in a nine-county Ulster it would have been only 55 per cent. Although unionists in the three excluded counties of Cavan, Monaghan and Donegal complained bitterly about being sacrificed, Northern Ireland leaders wanted a solid Protestant majority in order to establish the long-term security and safety of their new state.

This territorial arrangement was even more objectionable to the 450,000 Catholics (one-third of the population) who were incorporated into the new state against their wishes. There were nationalist majorities in the counties of Fermanagh and Tyrone, in the city of Derry and in Newry, and considerable nationalist numbers in north and west Belfast and south Armagh. Whilst desiring an independent united Ireland, many of these would have preferred continued direct rule from Britain to the new arrangements, and greatly resented their changed status as a powerless minority in a Protestant state dominated by their unionist opponents.

This solution which had been agreed at Westminster, therefore, left many people in Ulster angry and resentful. What seemed the simplest and quickest answer to politicians in Britain was not seen the same way in either part of Ireland. The unresolved question of the legitimacy of the state overrode all other political issues in Northern Ireland and meant that politics in the north, as in the south, developed in ways which were markedly different from most other European democracies. If the two communities were to enjoy their separate allegiances in peace, it was going to demand great tact, skill and tolerance from the new Northern Ireland government, and close supervision by the body with final responsibility for the new state, the United Kingdom parliament at Westminster.

However, the reality of British political life was that since the end of the First World War and the signing of the Versailles Treaty, Lloyd George's coalition government had been trying to distance itself from Ireland and the Irish problem. The government was deeply divided, including both home rulers and unionists among its leading members. The 1920–21 settlement which resulted in partition and the creation of two states was a compromise forced upon reluctant Ulster unionists and equally reluctant Irish nationalists. It certainly suited most members of the British government, in that it no longer directly ruled either part of Ireland, and the settlement effectively removed the irritant of Irish issues from British political life for the first time since 1800. It was not, however, a solution to the Irish question, the problematic terms of which now focused on Northern Ireland.

This desire to keep the Irish question at arm's length meant that British governments consistently declined to intervene in the internal politics of Northern Ireland until Harold Wilson's Labour government was reluctantly forced to send in troops as a result of the civil disturbances in August 1969. While this political stance was understandable from a British point of view, given the previous troubled history of entanglement, in the long run it amounted to a grievous abdication of responsibility, the repercussions of which became starkly obvious in the late 1960s.

The new state got off to a bad start, being born amidst sectarian violence, bloodshed and IRA attacks. Between July

1920 and July 1922 over 550 people died in inter-communal violence, with Catholics suffering most. Thousands of Catholics were driven out of their jobs and some twenty-three thousand forced out of their homes. All of this contributed to a deep sense of alienation felt by the Catholic minority, most of whom refused to recognise the new state. Nationalist MPs initially refused to sit in the new Northern Ireland parliament, so that at a time when the institutions of the new state were being formed, one-third of its citizens were refusing to participate in its structures. Although most nationalists eventually came to a reluctant acceptance of the state, they remained unwilling to participate actively, given the unionist establishment's distinct bias against a community which it viewed as the enemy within, a 'fifth column'. Thus, from the beginning many of the institutions were heavily weighted in favour of unionists, in whom one may see a sincere and continuing apprehension at the prospect of enforced union with the south.

The power of the Protestant majority was strengthened by the abolition of proportional representation in local (1922) and national (1929) elections and by the gerrymandering of constituency and local government boundaries, particularly in Derry city, to maintain unionist majorities. The Special Powers Act of 1922 gave to government extra-legal powers of arrest and imprisonment without trial, while an armed police force, backed up by an openly sectarian B Special reserve police, meant that constant control could be exercised over the suspect Catholic community.

Catholics responded by withdrawing into their own communities and creating their own socio-economic networks. Many took shelter within their religious associations and social and sporting fraternities. They harboured a bitter resentment against what they saw as the social and economic discrimination that was practised against them, particularly in the areas of public and private job allocation, and in local authority housing. Protestant supremacy in Northern Ireland was reinforced by this Catholic repudiation of the state. The character of life in both communities was parochial and partisan, and the deeply defensive nature of Northern Ireland unionists meant that its leaders were men who were dogged, conservative and narrow-minded, rather than outward-looking, imaginative and creative. The unionist domination of parliament meant that nationalists had no prospect of overturning the government, and therefore had little incentive to develop into a serious opposition with responsible policies of its own. The sectarian strife and turmoil which attended the inception of the state was to remain, and the close connection between security forces and the Protestant community revealed a fatal lack of consensus over the very existence of the state.

The heavy unemployment and social distress of the 1930s produced few examples of working-class solidarity across the religious divide, with the notable exception of the 1932 unemployment riots in Belfast which were non-sectarian in nature and for a brief moment united the Catholic working class of the Falls Road with the Protestant working class of the Shankill Road. More usually, the depression of the 1930s revealed the pernicious relationship between economic recession and sectarian violence. Widespread riots occurred in the early 1930s, reaching their peak in July and August 1935 when 13 people were killed, more than 600 wounded and over 2,000 driven from their homes. The comparative peacefulness of the next twenty-five years served only to disguise the inherent divisions of a fractured society.

Tensions between the north and the south continued throughout the Stormont years. In 1934 Prime Minister Craig, by then Lord Craigavon, famously boasted to the Northern Ireland House of Commons in the new parliament buildings at Stormont that 'we are a Protestant parliament and a Protestant state'. When challenged, he argued that this was merely a riposte to similar boasts in the south that it was a Catholic state for a Catholic people. Three years later, de Valera's new Irish constitution of 1937, with its distinctly republican and Catholic character, confirmed northern Protestant prejudices and reinforced their need to defend their existing institutions.

The war years brought new jobs and greater prosperity. This eased the sectarian tension, as did the shared experience of German bombing raids on Belfast. The number out of work fell from an average of 25 per cent in the 1930s to 5 per cent in 1942–45. Yet in good times as in bad, the level of unemployment in Northern Ireland remained substantially higher than in Britain. The shipbuilding, engineering and air-craft industries, which had been in decline, now made an important contribution to the United Kingdom's war effort. However, despite Craigavon's declaration that 'we are all King's men', the British government did not attempt to apply conscription to Northern Ireland, out of fear of the reaction this would provoke from nationalists.

The south's neutrality and its refusal to let Britain use its ports greatly increased Northern Ireland's strategic importance to Britain. Unionist fears of an ultimate British sell-out of the state to nationalist Ireland were given credence in June 1940 with the revelation that Churchill's government had made an offer to de Valera to support the principle of Irish unity in return for southern Ireland's support in the war. Craigavon declared that he was 'disgusted' by 'such treachery to loyal Ulster'. When the war ended, however, Churchill and most of the British political leadership felt they owed a debt to unionists for their loyalty, in contrast to their frustration at the southern government's neutrality. The war had led to very different experiences for the people of the north and the south and had reinforced the divisions between the two parts of Ireland, and between London and Dublin.

Craigavon died in 1940 and was succeeded as prime minister by J.M Andrews. After numerous criticisms about his effectiveness from his own party, Andrews was himself replaced three years later by Sir Basil Brooke, later Lord Brookeborough, who was to remain in office for twenty years. The new prime minister was initially alarmed at the advent in 1945 of a British Labour government under Clement Attlee (1883–1967), given Labour's traditional sympathy with the Irish nationalist cause. However, the unionist and Labour governments soon found little difficulty in working together. When the taoiseach, John A. Costello, announced his decision in 1948 to make the south a republic and withdraw from the Commonwealth, Northern Irish unionist interests and British defence interests coincided. The cabinet secretary, Norman Brooke, wrote: 'So far as can be foreseen it will never be to Great Britain's advantage that Northern Ireland should form part of a territory outside His Majesty's jurisdiction.' Attlee's Ireland Act of 1949, which was prompted by Costello's declaration of a republic, demonstrated Britain's new appreciation of Northern Ireland, by affirming that it would not cease to be part of the United Kingdom 'without the consent of the parliament of Northern Ireland'. This was the firmest guarantee that the unionists had ever won from Britain and effectively copper-fastened the existence of the Northern Irish state.

After 1945 the introduction to Northern Ireland of British welfare state measures benefited the poorer classes in society. The post-war years also saw a marked improvement in the prospects and conditions of the Catholic minority who were disproportionately represented among the unemployed and unskilled. Indeed northern Catholics became significantly better off than their co-religionists in the south. However, this improvement in many ways served to highlight other grievances such as voting iniquities, discrimination in employment and housing, and a general exclusion from political and economic power. Modernising welfare legislation came up against the sectarian parochialism of the past, to produce a combustible mixture which by the 1960s had grave implications for the stability of the state. The triumphalist and uncompromising behaviour of the unionist majority in the 1940s and 1950s did little to help reconcile nationalists to the 1920–21 settlement.

In the 1950s and 1960s, however, there was a growing tendency among Catholics to see their future within a Northern Ireland context rather than in an all-Ireland state. A new Catholic leadership was prepared to acquiesce in the constitutional status quo, with the proviso that Catholics received fairer treatment and were offered better opportunities. This was reflected in the failure of Operation Harvest, the violent IRA campaign of 1956–62 against British rule in Northern Ireland, which resulted in eighteen deaths. The aims of militant republicans seemed irrelevant to Catholics in the north and, in ending the campaign in 1962, the IRA blamed northern nationalists for not supporting it. It was soon to concentrate on achieving socialist objectives by political means, rather than Irish unity by military means.

The 1960s began as a decade of hope. In the south the aged figure of de Valera had been replaced by a much more dynamic leader in Sean Lemass. In the north the increasingly ineffective premiership of Basil Brooke came to an end. His continuing failure to promote economic development led to the moderate unionist Captain Terence O'Neill (1914–90) being appointed prime minister in 1963. O'Neill hoped to modernise Northern Ireland by improving its economic performance and by 'building bridges between the two traditions' in the north. He also believed that reconciliation between the Republic and the north was necessary for progress, and was prepared to move away from the siege mentality of many of those unionists who had been associated with the formation of the state. However, there were numerous obstacles to change in both communities in the north, and the ancient divisions in the region survived intact.

O'Neill's most dramatic gesture was his invitation to Sean Lemass to visit Northern Ireland in January 1965, the first such meeting for forty years. He also encouraged economic collaboration and cross-border co-operation. However, O'Neill's modest reform proposals alarmed many traditional unionists, some of whom gathered around the imposing figure of Ian Paisley (1926–), leader of the Free Presbyterian Church. They began to campaign under the slogan 'O'Neill must go'. In the meantime, many younger Catholics wished to abandon the policy of remaining aloof from the state which had been followed since 1921, seeking instead to play a greater role in political life in order to achieve equal citizenship within Northern Ireland. A much larger, ambitious, educated Catholic middle class had emerged whose aims were not to overthrow the state but rather to reform its structures and institutions by applying British standards of justice. It rapidly became dissatisfied with the gap between O'Neill's actual performance and his gestures, many of which seemed merely cosmetic. In 1967 the Northern Ireland Civil Rights Association was formed, inspired by the American civil rights campaign of Martin Luther King, and began a peaceful campaign of street protests and demonstrations to end discriminatory practices.

Most of these events went unnoticed in Britain and attracted only sporadic attention from Wilson's Labour government, until the media began to pay increasing attention to rising sectarian tension. In October 1968 the Northern Ireland government banned a proposed civil rights march in Derry. The march went ahead and there was a violent clash with the police, who were widely criticised for the unrestrained batoning of unarmed demonstrators. As television images of the incident flashed across the world, the sectarian flame was reignited and community relations dramatically deteriorated. It soon became apparent that a new version of the Irish question was emerging, successive British governments having for too long neglected their responsibilities. Labour ministers belatedly came to realise the seriousness of the situation, and saw that if it deteriorated further they would be dragged in. O'Neill made a television broadcast on 9 December 1968, beginning with the ominous statement, 'Ulster stands at the crossroads'. He continued: 'What kind of Ulster do you want? A happy respected province ... or a place continually torn apart by riots and demonstrations, and regarded by the rest of Britain as a political outcast?' In 1968 few realised how long and painful would be the road upon which Northern Ireland was about to embark.

13

TRANSFORMATION AND MODERNISATION
IN THE REPUBLIC
1959–1998

The year 1959, which saw the appointment of Sean Lemass (1899–1971) as taoiseach, is widely regarded as the *annus mirabilis* of modern Ireland, the date which marks the beginning of the belated economic modernisation of the nation. In place of de Valera's vision of a rural, introspective, self-sufficient Gaelic idyll, the pragmatic Lemass, who retained power until 1966, envisaged an industrialised, entrepreneurial, outward-looking meritocratic society. The blueprint for this new Ireland was supplied by the influential secretary of the department of finance, T.K. Whitaker, whose 1958 report entitled *Economic Development* formed the basis for Lemass's ground-breaking First Programme for Economic Expansion of the same year. This was a five-year plan (1958–63) for economic expansion which emphasised the need to replace the protectionist principles of previous decades with free-trade policies, increase state investment in productive enterprises and attract international investment in export-oriented Irish industries. By the end of 1960, Lemass was presiding over a rapidly expanding economy characterised by rising industrial growth rates and falling levels of unemployment and emigration.

Efficiency and competitiveness became the new watchwords as tariff barriers were dismantled, access to international markets sought and capital grants and tax concessions offered to foreign firms. An eagerness to engage in European economic co-operation was signalled by Ireland's application in 1961 for membership of the European Economic Community, to which it eventually gained admittance in 1973. Meanwhile, two economic agreements with Britain (the 1960 Anglo-Irish trade pact and the 1965 Anglo-Irish Free Trade Area Agreement) paved the way for full free trade between the two countries by 1975. There was, as a 1960s *Time* magazine feature on Ireland proclaimed, 'New Spirit in the Oul Sod'.

This radical redirection of economic policy produced dramatic results over the next decade as over three hundred foreign-owned companies were established nationwide, national income rose, unemployment fell, emigration slowed dramatically, the Republic's population increased and the material prosperity of the majority of its citizens leapt to unprecedented heights. Sweeping social and cultural change paralleled this sudden economic expansion. Increased affluence fuelled a growth in materialism which was fed in turn by the nation's exposure to the glitzy international world of consumer capitalism through the rise of tourism and foreign travel, the relaxation of the film and book censorship laws and the advent in 1961 of that most potent agent of cultural change, television.

Telefís Éireann played a major part in accelerating the trend towards liberalism in 1960s Ireland. Innovative home-made programmes, such as the talk show the *Late Late Show*, provided a forum for the public discussion of hitherto taboo subjects (especially those relating to sexual morality) and in the process subjected the values, attitudes and often the representatives of traditional Ireland to close critical scrutiny. Indeed, so concerned was one reactionary Irish politician by the corrosive influence of such programmes on the moral fabric of the nation that he boldly proclaimed that 'there was no sex in Ireland before television'! The dismay of Irish traditionalists was further deepened by the social radicalism of the Second Vatican Council (1962–65). The innovations of Pope John XXIII sent shock waves through the conservative Irish Church and set it on a turbulent course of readjustment to the unpropitious realities of an increasingly secular and sceptical social order.

In the diplomatic sphere, the later years of Lemass's premiership were marked by a historic breakthrough in relations between the Republic and Northern Ireland. In January and February 1965, as has been seen, Lemass officially met his northern counterpart, Captain Terence O'Neill, first in Belfast and then in Dublin, to discuss matters of mutual economic concern, a symbolic encounter ending a forty-year cold war between the two governments. But while this new spirit of *rapprochement* was broadly welcomed in the south, O'Neill's conciliatory diplomacy, coupled with his mildly reformist social policies, alienated many conservative Ulster Unionists and ultimately led to the splitting of unionism into 'official' and 'unofficial' strands.

The year 1966 brought Ireland's political and cultural divisions into fresh focus as nationalists and unionists celebrated the fiftieth anniversaries of two glorious events in their respective historical traditions, namely, the Easter Rising and the heroic sacrifice of the Ulster Division at the Battle of the Somme.

Though none could have known it at the time, two other events of that year, each in their way legacies of 1916 – the blowing up of the memorial to Admiral Nelson in Dublin by the IRA and the shooting of four Catholic men (two of them dead) in Belfast by the revived Protestant paramilitary group the UVF – were ominous portents of the violent re-eruption of ancient antagonisms which were to engulf Northern Ireland before the decade was out.

The onerous political responsibility for responding to the northern Troubles and managing their impact on the southern state fell to Jack Lynch (1917–), the mild-mannered Corkman who succeeded Lemass as taoiseach in 1966. The arrival of British troops on the streets of Derry and Belfast in August 1969, albeit to an initial welcome from the minority Catholic community, coupled with the sight of refugees streaming into makeshift shelters in the Republic, shattered southern complacency and reignited smouldering nationalist resentments within the republican ranks of Lynch's Fianna Fáil government. Following an initial implied threat to intervene to defend Catholics against Protestant attack, Lynch pledged his government to a more realistic policy of peaceful resolution of the northern problem, while retaining a long-term aspiration to Irish unity.

His moderate stance did not receive universal cabinet support, however, as the dramatic events of May 1970 were to prove. In that month two senior ministers, Neil Blaney and Charles Haughey (1925–), were sacked from the Irish government and charged with conspiring to import arms and ammunition into the Republic for use in the north. Although the 'arms crisis', as it was known, ended with the acquittal of both men, the ability of Lynch's government to contain political violence was tested repeatedly throughout the tumultuous early seventies, most notably after the introduction of internment in August 1971 and in the emotional aftermath of Bloody Sunday in Derry in January 1972. Southern revulsion at the killing of thirteen unarmed civilians by British paratroopers in Derry city resulted in the burning of the British embassy in Dublin following an angry mass demonstration on 2 February. It was now clear that the northern Troubles, which will be discussed in detail in Chapters 14 and 15, were putting Anglo-Irish relations under intense strain.

As civil conflict intensified north of the border, the Republic joined the EEC in January 1973 along with Britain and Denmark, thus placing the northern issue within a broader diplomatic setting. The immediate material effects of membership were muted by the fact that the Republic's accession coincided with the first major economic recession of the seventies induced by the 1973 Middle East oil crisis. When the crisis abated, however, it became clear that membership of the EEC was having a transformative socio-economic impact on the country. The expansion of trade links with its European partners reduced the nation's economic dependence on Britain and the psychological baggage that went with it. A new economic self-confidence manifested itself in the Republic's decision to join the European Monetary System in 1979, while Britain stayed out. European grants and subsidies greatly benefited the Irish agricultural sector, while the application of European laws improved workers' rights and promoted greater social tolerance. Overall, Ireland's positive experience of EC membership has engendered strong pro-European loyalties in the majority of its citizens, in marked contrast to the Euro-sceptical attitudes of many Britons.

In 1973 Fianna Fáil was replaced in office after sixteen years by a Fine Gael–Labour coalition government led by Liam Cosgrave (1920–), son of the first Irish prime minister. Cosgrave continued Lynch's northern policy of quiet diplomacy. The high watermark of his government's influence on Northern Irish affairs came at the Sunningdale Conference of 1973. The Dublin delegation secured a formal acceptance by both British and Northern Irish representatives of a southern Irish dimension in the future government of the region, in return for which Cosgrave agreed that any change in the status of Northern Ireland must have the consent of the majority there. However, the proposed instrument of southern influence, a Council of Ireland to deal with matters of mutual concern in the island as a whole, never materialised and disappeared from the political agenda following the collapse of the northern power-sharing Executive in May 1974.

During the mid-1970s, Cosgrave's coalition government was beset by a series of threats to internal state security from both loyalist and republican paramilitaries. Among the most alarming incidents were the killing of thirty-three people by loyalist car bombs in Dublin and Monaghan in May 1974, the greatest loss of life in any one day of the Troubles; the IRA kidnapping of Dutch industrialist, Tiede Herrema, in 1975; the unrest generated by the death in an English prison of republican hunger-striker, Frank Stagg, the following year; and the IRA assassination of the British ambassador, Christopher Ewart-Biggs, in July 1976.

The last atrocity prompted the government to declare a state of national emergency and introduce an Emergency Powers Bill to permit the detention of terrorist suspects for seven days without charge. This draconian legislation mirrored the Prevention of Terrorism Act, which was hurriedly introduced in Britain and Northern Ireland following the Birmingham pub bombings in November 1974. The Irish legislation proved much more controversial, however. The decision of the president, Cearbhall Ó Dálaigh, to refer the Bill to the Supreme Court to test its constitutionality drew the public wrath of the

Irish defence minister Patrick Donegan, whose description of Ó Dálaigh as a 'thundering disgrace' precipitated a dramatic constitutional crisis which resulted in the president's resignation in October 1976.

In June 1977 Fianna Fáil returned to power with its biggest ever parliamentary majority. Two years later, Lynch resigned as taoiseach and was succeeded by Charles Haughey, whose appointment occurred within months of Margaret Thatcher (1925–) becoming Britain's first female prime minister. The accession to power of these two charismatic and controversial leaders heralded the dawn of a new phase in Anglo-Irish relations which was characterised by an inter-governmental approach to Northern Ireland based on a growing recognition by both the British and Irish governments of the failure of internal initiatives to resolve the Troubles. The search for new institutional structures began with a meeting of the new premiers in May 1980 and was advanced at the first summit meeting between them in Dublin in December, at which they agreed to establish joint Anglo-Irish studies groups to explore matters of common concern. Although the constitutional position of the north was not discussed at this meeting, they did agree to examine 'the totality of relationships within these islands' at their next meeting in 1981.

By then, however, relations between London and Dublin had deteriorated because of Britain's inept handling of the Maze hunger strikes. Diplomatic coolness hardened into outright estrangement in the spring of 1982, when the Irish government refused to support Britain's military conflict with Argentina over the Falkland Islands on the grounds that to do so would endanger Ireland's traditional policy of neutrality. Anglo-Irish relations remained strained until the autumn of 1983, by which time Haughey's Fianna Fáil government had been replaced by another Fine Gael–Labour coalition under the premiership of Garret FitzGerald (1926–).

Unlike Haughey, whose republican rhetoric alienated many northern unionists, FitzGerald aspired to a pluralist unitary state to be achieved by consent, in which the cultural identities and religious convictions of all the people of Ireland would be afforded equality of status and mutual respect. Prompted by Northern Ireland's Social Democratic and Labour Party leader John Hume (1937–), he set about convening an all-Ireland conference in early 1983 to consider how such a state might be achieved. The result was the New Ireland Forum, which met for the first time at Dublin Castle in May 1983. Over the next twelve months representatives of constitutional nationalist parties from both parts of Ireland deliberated on the shape of a new Ireland.

The resultant Forum report recommended a unitary state as the preferred option, while retaining joint Irish–British authority over Northern Ireland and some form of federal or confederal state as possible alternatives. Despite the fact that all three options were brusquely dismissed by Mrs Thatcher following an Anglo-Irish summit at Chequers in November 1984, the report set the political agenda for a process of patient diplomacy between Irish and British government ministers and their civil servants which culminated in the signing of the Anglo-Irish Agreement by the two premiers at Hillsborough Castle, County Down, on 15 November 1985.

The agreement, the most historic Anglo-Irish accord since the 1921 treaty, granted the Irish government a consultative role in certain stated aspects of Northern Ireland affairs through an inter-governmental conference, serviced by a secretariat staffed by civil servants from both countries, based at Maryfield near Belfast. If this measure boosted the hopes of northern nationalists that their interests and aspirations might be advanced, the two governments' affirmation of the majority's right to decide on the constitutional future of Northern Ireland was intended to allay unionist fears of forcible absorption into a united Ireland. Such reassurance fell on deaf ears, however, as an outraged unionist community proclaimed its vehement opposition to the agreement through street demonstrations, civil disobedience and acts of intimidation and violence. Sustained unionist opposition continued over the next three years, yet failed to weaken the two governments' resolve to implement the terms of the agreement, and so avoided a repeat of the collapse of the 1974 power-sharing experiment.

Despite the diplomatic success of the Hillsborough accord, the late 1980s proved to be a time of recurring tensions in Anglo-Irish relations. Charles Haughey's return to power in 1987 coincided with a period of renewed controversy over the extradition of terrorist suspects from the Republic to face charges in Britain and Northern Ireland. A number of highly publicised cases of Irish courts' refusal to extradite suspects, for diverse reasons, led to mutual recriminations between Dublin and London. Relations were further strained by Irish disquiet over the British judiciary's inequitable treatment of Irish people as exemplified by the release on appeal of the Guildford Four, Birmingham Six and Maguire Seven, all of whom had been wrongfully imprisoned for terrorist offences in the 1970s. Matters began to improve in the 1990s, however, helped by the personal friendship which developed between the two new premiers, John Major (1943–) and Albert Reynolds (1932–), and the emergence of a mutual desire to bring about a peaceful settlement in Northern Ireland.

In the internal politics of the Republic, the 1980s were punctuated by a number of bitterly acrimonious debates between liberals and traditionalists about the social and moral direction of Irish society. The visit of Pope John Paul II to Ireland in 1979, during which he condemned secular materialism and reaffirmed traditional Catholic family values, reinvigorated the forces of moral conservatism and triggered a mood of Catholic revivalism. However, advocates of greater social pluralism found a powerful ally in Garret FitzGerald, who in September 1981 launched a 'constitutional crusade' to create 'a genuine republic on the principles of Tone and Davis'. He criticised the sectarian nature of the Republic's constitution and laws and spoke of the need to make the south more acceptable to northern unionists. His liberal agenda drew the wrath of many conservative Catholics, however, and worried some members of the hierarchy.

The first test of strength between the forces of liberalism and conservatism resulted in a victory for the latter when a constitutional referendum to prohibit abortion was passed by a majority of two to one in September 1983. Undaunted by this defeat and the divisiveness it engendered, FitzGerald continued to promote liberal social reforms throughout the rest of his premiership. In February 1985 his coalition government succeeded in passing a Bill to legalise the sale of contraceptives to adults, despite opposition from Catholic traditionalists. The following year the government introduced a Bill to remove the constitutional ban on civil divorce, but this was comprehensively rejected in a referendum in June 1986. A disappointed FitzGerald admitted that the outcome was 'a setback to the long-term prospect of the two parts of Ireland coming closer together politically' and a rebuff to northern unionists.

The liberal cause received a significant symbolic boost in 1990, however, when the feminist lawyer Mary Robinson (1944–), who had earlier resigned from the Labour Party in protest against the Anglo-Irish Agreement being imposed upon unwilling unionists, became Ireland's first female president. Her victory was widely seen both as a triumph for the advocates of a secular, pluralist agenda and as a striking assertion of the public identity of Irish women, for so long silenced and marginalised in society. Women's political prominence was further enhanced when a record number of female candidates (twenty) was elected to the Dáil in the 1992 general election. As Robinson herself memorably declared in her victory speech, the hand that rocked the cradle was now rocking the system.

The 1980s was a difficult decade for the Irish economy. The recession triggered by a further oil crisis in 1979 was compounded by reckless government borrowing, leading to increased levels of unemployment and emigration, particularly among the young, many of whom went to Britain. There was a corresponding rise in urban poverty and criminal activity, much of it drug-related, as Dublin earned an unwanted reputation as 'the heroin capital of Europe'. Ten years later, however, Ireland was projecting an altogether different international image.

As the 1990s unfolded, tangible signs that Irish society was becoming more liberal emerged. In 1992 the laws on abortion were modified in the aftermath of the infamous 'X' case, in which a fourteen-year-old rape victim was initially prevented by a court injunction from travelling to Britain to have an abortion. Homosexuality was decriminalised in 1993, and two years later a second referendum to remove the constitutional prohibition on divorce received the assent of the electorate, albeit by the narrowest of margins. But perhaps the most striking feature of Irish life in the 1990s was the degree to which public confidence in the moral and political authority of the institutions of Church and state was profoundly undermined by a series of crises and controversies.

A number of financial scandals in the Irish business world in the early part of the decade was followed by a lengthy tribunal of inquiry into the beef processing industry which uncovered evidence of fraud and corruption involving businessmen and government ministers. The weakening of the authority of the Catholic Church has been marked by equally dramatic public scandals. In May 1992 the Bishop of Galway, Eamonn Casey, was forced to resign following the revelation that he had fathered a son by an American divorcée in the 1970s and used Church funds to pay for his upkeep. Two years later, a crisis over the extradition to Northern Ireland of a paedophile priest who had for years been protected from civil prosecution by the Church authorities led to the collapse of the Fianna Fáil–Labour coalition government. A national survey carried out in the aftermath of this collapse showed that the overwhelming majority of respondents believed that a 'sleaze factor' had now entered Irish politics. Revelations of an even more tumultuous nature emerged in the summer of 1997, when a government tribunal of inquiry into payments to politicians found that the former taoiseach, Charles Haughey, had accepted secret financial gifts from a millionaire Irish businessman which he had failed to disclose.

The cumulative effect of these controversies was to raise fundamental questions about the nature and practice of democracy in contemporary Ireland, questions which inevitably engendered cynicism in the minds of many Irish people, young and old. Paradoxically, such alienation from the democratic process in the Republic coincided with a renewed momentum towards democracy in Northern Ireland, generated by the peace process. This is one of the many curious paradoxes that characterise a society in which the forces of rapid change have produced an uneasy contiguity of the traditional and the modern or, as some would have it, the post-modern.

In another of those stray coincidences that retrospectively acquire symbolic significance, the day of the IRA cease-fire in Northern Ireland, 31 August 1994, was also the day on which the investment bank Morgan Stanley favourably compared the Republic's thriving economy with the East Asian 'tiger' economies, thereby launching the concept of the 'Celtic tiger'. The country's recent economic performance has been truly remarkable. For several years in the 1990s, Ireland's economic growth rates have been among the highest in the world, averaging at over 7 per cent per annum in the late 1990s. By the end of 1996 the Republic was producing more wealth per head of population than the United Kingdom and could boast the highest growth rate in the EU, having met most of the Maastricht criteria for European monetary union. Manufacturing production, especially in the computer and electronics industry, flourished and foreign investment increased substantially, leading to higher incomes and increased job opportunities. National income rose by 44 per cent between 1993 and 1998, with a corresponding rapid rise in living standards. Inflation is low, the national debt is falling annually, the public finances are healthy, export growth is strong and profits are booming. For the first time since the 1970s, the Republic experienced net immigration, with many former emigrants among those eager to enjoy the benefits of the Irish economic miracle.

Not surprisingly, Ireland's unprecedented recent economic success has generated a national mood of ebullient self-confidence and a cultural vibrancy that has made the country a most popular European tourist destination. Not only this, Irish culture at the end of the century has become increasingly internationalised through the work of writers like Seamus Heaney and Roddy Doyle, the films of Neil Jordan and Jim Sheridan, the music of U2, the spectacular Irish dance show *Riverdance*, and what is perhaps the most incongruous example of reverse colonisation, the Irish theme pub.

Yet alluring though the Celtic tiger's stripes may be, there is a dark underbelly. Ireland's sudden economic prosperity has meant little for many sections of the population. Thousands continue to live below the poverty line and problems of long-term unemployment and social inequality remain stubbornly persistent. Soaring levels of violent and organised crime have led to the introduction of a panoply of anti-crime measures, the harshest of which are designed to combat the rise in drug trafficking. Moreover, the country's improved economic situation has made it attractive to asylum seekers and refugees, whose arrival has prompted the implementation of some of the toughest immigration controls in Western Europe. At a more fundamental level, nagging doubts remain about the sustainability of Irish economic growth, given its heavy reliance on foreign capital rather than an indigenous industrial base. In all of this, the paradoxes resonate: a nation whose history is defined by the experience of emigration, which has scattered its citizens all over the globe, is now showing itself reluctant to receive the scatterings of others, at a time when its national prosperity is being underwritten by transnational wealth.

Nevertheless the mood of the nation remains overwhelmingly buoyant as the new millennium approaches, even if Ireland's cosmopolitan present sometimes looks more like its confessional past. This was nowhere more evident than in the controversy caused by President Mary McAleese (1951–) when, within weeks of her inauguration, she accepted communion at a Church of Ireland ceremony in Dublin in December 1997. Whereas her action was forthrightly condemned by some senior Catholic churchmen who regarded it as a blatant breach of canon law, many ordinary Irish people took a less dogmatic view. To them, the president's gesture represented a welcome act of ecumenism and a tangible expression of her genuine desire to 'build bridges' with other religious traditions on the island. To see it as such is to hope that the deep divisions of the past might yet be healed by future dialogue and understanding, and that the process of peace and justice in Ireland might be spiritual as well as political, personal as well as formal.

14

POLITICAL VIOLENCE IN
NORTHERN IRELAND
1969–1993

In the winter of 1968–69 the Northern Ireland prime
minister, Terence O'Neill, came under increasing pressure
from three sources. First, the predominantly Catholic civil
rights movement was demanding widespread reform of the
state to end the gerrymandering of electoral boundaries, to al-
locate local authority housing on a fair basis, to disband the B
Specials and to introduce 'one man, one vote' in local council
elections. Second, there was a growing number of unionist
critics of O'Neill, the most extreme of whom was Ian Paisley,
who feared that O'Neill's concessions to the nationalist minority were weakening the unionist position. Third, Wilson's
Labour government was beginning to grow more concerned
about the increasing unrest in Northern Ireland.

On 4 January 1969 a march from Belfast to Derry organised
by students at Queen's University Belfast and other civil rights
supporters was attacked by some two hundred loyalists,

including members of the B Specials. That night, amid widespread unrest in Derry, the police went on the rampage in the Catholic Bogside area of the city. Sectarian passions were now rising to a level unknown for many years and undermining any goodwill that O'Neill's modest reforms had earned him from the nationalist population. Ultra-loyalists like Paisley and some within O'Neill's own party saw the civil rights movement as a republican plot aimed at bringing down the northern state, not merely reforming it. In desperation, O'Neill called a general election in February, hoping to strengthen his hand, but the splits within unionism widened, and his own position was further undermined by the relative success of more hardline loyalist candidates. Of the 52 seats in the Stormont parliament, unionists won 39, but 10 of these went to anti-O'Neillites, with 2 undecided. O'Neill resigned in April, a beaten man, to be replaced as prime minister by his cousin, the lacklustre James Chichester-Clark (1923–). To add insult to injury, O'Neill's seat at the subsequent by-election was won by his arch-enemy, Paisley.

Sectarian clashes grew more frequent during the summer of 1969. British civil servants sent over to Belfast from London to oversee reforms were totally unfamiliar with the political culture, historical complexities and sectarian passions which confronted them. The heightened tension during the traditional Orange marches in July led to rioting in Belfast, but the climactic moment of no return occurred in Derry in August, following disturbances during a Protestant Apprentice Boys' march in the city. The B Specials played a critical role in these events. They attempted to enter the Catholic Bogside area but were prevented by the residents who, believing that their homes were about to be attacked, erected barricades and hurled petrol bombs at the police. Three days of serious rioting followed, and this spread to Belfast where Protestant mobs attacked Catholic areas of the city, sometimes assisted by armed B Specials.

It was soon clear that the Northern Ireland police was incapable of subduing the violence and maintaining law and order. During the night of 14 August, six people died as a result of the riots and over four hundred houses were severely damaged. On the same date, the Labour government reluctantly took the decision to send in British troops to restore order. They were greeted warmly by the Catholic population, who saw them as saviours, infinitely preferable to the armed police, while Protestants looked on hesitantly, realising that the unionist regime was no longer sole master of its own house.

The presence of British troops on the streets of Belfast and Derry was to change fundamentally the nature of the Northern Ireland problem. Having ignored the state it created for almost fifty years, an ill-prepared British government was now dragged into its affairs, with little thought being given to the long-term implications. There was uncertainty amongst all groups as to whether the army was there to protect the Catholic population, to subdue revolution, or to shore up a discredited regime. The officer commanding British troops, Lieutenant-General Sir Ian Freeland, perceptively warned that the initial 'honeymoon period between troops and the local people is likely to be short-lived'.

Wilson's government, which now had effective overall responsibility for maintaining order, continued to work through the unionist government at Stormont in the unrealistic hope of keeping the northern problem at a distance. The expectation was that the army would be able to keep the peace while some reforms were made to the running of the state, and that normality would resume under a reorganised unionist government. However, the short-term reforms which Wilson's government forced the Northern Ireland administration to concede only served to antagonise further many Protestants, and failed to reconcile Catholics, a growing number of whom were coming to regard Northern Ireland as a 'failed political entity' and to see their security in a new united Ireland.

The IRA had been much criticised in some nationalist areas for its failure to defend besieged Catholic communities during the rioting of August 1969. In January 1970 it split into two groups. The Official IRA, the so-called 'Red' faction, retained its socialist objectives, but a breakaway group, the Provisional or 'Green' IRA, soon became the dominant body. The movement quickly established itself in Catholic housing estates and spent much of 1970 training its volunteers and acquiring weapons. The Provisionals' aim was to drive the old enemy, the British army, out of Northern Ireland and to bring about the unification which had been denied them in 1921.

Gradually, the IRA began to attack British troops, with the first soldier being killed in February 1971. By this time the Labour government had been replaced by Edward Heath's Conservative administration, which tended to see the IRA as the basic problem, together with the Catholic community which gave it active or tacit support. This new emphasis on a security response to what was a political problem further alienated Catholics from the British government and its unionist allies at Stormont, and led to the army being perceived in Catholic areas as an army of occupation, which was exactly what the Provisionals were arguing.

In August 1971 the London government made the disastrous decision to accept the Northern Ireland government's advice and introduce internment without trial. Internment was very much a one-sided operation against the nationalist population. No loyalists were included among the 342 men arrested. Many innocent people were detained, internees were brutalised and tortured, violence escalated and

Catholic disenchantment deepened. Indeed Catholic and Protestant fears were such that there was a massive movement of people to 'safe areas', producing the largest enforced population movement in Europe since 1945. The final straw came on 30 January 1972 when British paratroops killed thirteen unarmed civilians during a civil rights march in Derry, on what became known as Bloody Sunday. These killings, for which Britain was heavily criticised in the international media, led to a wave of anger and revulsion amongst the Catholic community in the north. The British government, having tried to work through the Stormont regime, finally realised that it would have to accept full responsibility for policy in Northern Ireland. Accordingly, in March 1972 Heath's government suspended the Stormont parliament and established direct rule from London through a Northern Ireland secretary of state.

Although initially intended as a temporary measure, direct rule was to become a permanent feature of the state. Unionists were shocked at the removal of what they regarded as their parliament, and felt a deep sense of betrayal by the British government, especially a Conservative one, given the close alliance between British conservatism and Ulster unionism for most of the previous eighty years. Many unionists, moreover, regarded the fall of Stormont as a victory for the Provisional IRA, a perception which deepened their insecurity about their political future and led to the formation of a number of paramilitary organisations in Protestant working-class districts to counteract the activities of the Provisionals and carry out attacks on Catholic areas. As the IRA increased its campaign of shootings and bombings, 1972 became the most violent year of the Troubles, with 467 deaths in Northern Ireland, 321 of which were civilian casualties.

Catholic political self-confidence was growing, particularly as the British government was coming to accept the fact that

the nationalists' aspiration towards unity required formal ac-
knowledgement, and that the Dublin government might in
some way be involved in an overall solution. The core problem for the British government, however, was how to reconcile the opposing interests of nationalists and unionists. In both
groups there were different factions. Within nationalism, those
republicans represented by Sinn Féin saw the British presence
as the key problem and refused to participate in constitutional
politics, while more moderate nationalists, represented by
the Social Democratic and Labour Party, were willing to
co-operate with the government to reform the northern state.
Within unionism, extreme loyalist groups objected to concessions to nationalists, and to the involvement of the Dublin
government in northern affairs, which they considered would
weaken the link with Britain.

For a great many years, Northern Ireland unionists had co-
operated so closely with British Conservatives that they were,
for practical purposes, one party. In the early 1970s, however,
the unionists broke this alliance and became a separate force in
United Kingdom politics. In 1971 the previously monolithic
Ulster Unionist Party split when Ian Paisley broke away to
form the Democratic Unionist Party. The DUP, although
smaller in numbers than the 'official' unionists, was dominated
by the imposing figure of Paisley and adopted extreme positions on most matters. Its roots were more working class than
those of the Ulster Unionists, and its members tended on the
whole to be Presbyterian, while the 'officials' represented a
broader range of Protestantism, including a higher proportion
of members of the Church of Ireland. Despite these cleavages
of class and religion, both parties remained firmly wedded to
the Union, as the results of a 1973 plebiscite on the border issue
confirmed. Although nationalists were advised to abstain,
almost all of the 58 per cent of the electorate who voted

supported the status quo.

By 1972 it was apparent to the British government that military measures alone could not solve the problem and so during the next twenty-five years a series of political initiatives was attempted. All of these took place against a background of killings and bombings in Northern Ireland and Britain, while successive governments sought to contain the political violence through emergency legislation. The first major initiative took place in November 1973 when the British government, while guaranteeing Northern Ireland's position in the United Kingdom, proposed to set up an elected Executive in which power was to be shared by moderate unionists and nationalists. A Council of Ireland was also proposed, which would allow Dublin an ill-defined role in Northern Ireland affairs.

There was, however, much unionist opposition to these proposals, and in particular to the Council of Ireland, which was seen as a threat to the Union. Amid increasing unrest, groups of loyalist workers, calling themselves the Ulster Workers' Council, declared a general strike in May 1974. They were aided by loyalist paramilitary groups such as the Ulster Defence Association. Despite widespread intimidation, Wilson's new Labour government was unwilling to use the army to break the strike and support the power-sharing Executive. The result was the ignominious collapse of the five-month-old Executive on 28 May 1974, and a confirmation of loyalists' belief that they could effectively destroy by force any political plan put forward by Britain which they opposed.

For the rest of the 1970s there was little sense of plan or purpose to British policy in Northern Ireland, but rather a further emphasis on security measures. In 1973 the IRA took its bombing campaign to England. Following major bombings in London, Guildford and Birmingham, the Labour government rushed through the Prevention of Terrorism Act in 1974, part of which enabled the authorities to ban suspected terrorists from entry into Britain and to banish them to Northern Ireland, although it was still an integral part of the United Kingdom. Within Northern Ireland itself, the mid-1970s saw an increasingly vicious series of bombings and 'tit-for-tat' sectarian murders. In an attempt to restore the appearance of normality, the British government adopted a new strategy of 'Ulsterisation' in 1976, whereby the prominent role of the army was replaced by an emphasis on the primacy of the RUC.

In 1976 'special category' (political) status for paramilitary prisoners was also removed in an attempt to criminalise those convicted of political offences. This move precipitated a grave crisis in the prisons which came to dominate northern politics in the late 1970s. Republican prisoners, demanding political status, went on a 'blanket protest', later followed by a 'dirty protest'. These involved prisoners refusing to wear prison clothes or clean out their cells. Finally, in March 1981, they began a series of hunger strikes in their H-block cells in the Maze prison near Belfast in order to regain political status. The hunger strikes provided a huge public platform for the Provisional movement, and its political wing, Sinn Féin, achieved worldwide publicity when the leader of the hunger-strikers, Bobby Sands, was elected to Westminster in April. His election revealed levels of support amongst the nationalist community far beyond that usually associated with revolutionary republicanism. The prolonged fasting and dramatic deaths of Sands and nine other hunger-strikers later in 1981 further increased the publicity for republicans in America and Europe, and greatly increased the level of their support from nationalists, as evidenced by the election of Sands's election agent, Owen Carron, in August 1981.

The Conservative prime minister, Margaret Thatcher, leader of the government elected in 1979, was determined not to give in to the pressure exerted by the hunger-strikers and their supporters. She resisted their demands until they finally capitulated, but this was a classic case of winning a battle yet losing the war. Britain's handling of the affair was disastrous. It encouraged the Provisionals to attempt to capitalise on their increased support by entering the political arena and contesting elections. The new republican strategy was aimed at taking power in Ireland 'with a ballot box in one hand and an Armalite in the other'. The growing success of Sinn Féin at both local and national elections led to government fears that the moderate SDLP would be replaced as the main voice of Catholic nationalism in Northern Ireland. These fears were increased when Sinn Féin leader Gerry Adams (1948–) won the West Belfast seat in the Westminster general election of June 1983. As political agreement between the parties within Northern Ireland seemed impossible, Britain looked to the Irish government to share the problem, and sought to find agreement between the two governments on the way forward.

On the surface, the period between 1980 and 1985 was a time of little political progress in Anglo-Irish relations. There was a number of public disagreements between the two governments, including an angry confrontation over Britain's conduct of the Falklands War. Relations were further soured in October 1984, when there was an almost successful IRA attempt to assassinate Margaret Thatcher and members of her cabinet during the Conservative Party conference in Brighton. Five people were killed when a bomb exploded in the Grand Hotel, including an MP and the wife of the government chief whip. British public opinion was outraged at this atrocity, the dreadful reality of which showed just how close the IRA had come to wiping out most of the British cabinet. Behind the scenes, however, officials of both governments had been co-operating to produce the historic agreement which was signed by the two premiers at Hillsborough Castle on 15 November 1985.

The Anglo-Irish Agreement, whilst guaranteeing that Northern Ireland would remain part of the United Kingdom as long as a majority of the population so desired, had the fundamental importance of granting Dublin a permanent consultative role in the affairs of Northern Ireland for the first time since 1921. This willingness to share decision-making powers with the southern government marked a decisive shift in British government thinking. Republicans opposed the agreement because of its continuing support for the Northern Irish state, while unionists were outraged at the way they had been excluded from the two governments' negotiations. In December 1985 all fifteen unionist MPs resigned their Westminster seats in order to fight anti-agreement by-election campaigns under the slogan 'Ulster says no!' The following March, a unionist 'Day of Action' brought the province to a standstill. The agreement, however, was widely welcomed in the rest of Ireland, Britain and the international world. Despite the widespread, prolonged, and sometimes violent loyalist opposition, the agreement remained secure. This time the British government did not capitulate to loyalist opposition as it had done in 1974.

Despite this inter-governmental consensus, violence still occupied the centre stage. Allegations of a 'shoot-to-kill' policy by the security forces in Northern Ireland were followed by a huge IRA bomb in Enniskillen on Remembrance Day, November 1987, which killed eleven civilians and left over sixty injured. There were also increased killings by Protestant paramilitaries, and three unarmed IRA volunteers were shot dead by British soldiers in Gibraltar in March 1988. However, the appointment of Peter Brooke as Northern Ireland secretary of state in July 1989 produced a fresh political initiative.

Shortly after taking office, Brooke made a number of important speeches in which he indicated that the government would talk to Sinn Féin if the IRA renounced violence; that Britain's role in Northern Ireland was a neutral one; and that Britain would accept Irish unification if a majority of the people in Northern Ireland consented to it. Since 1988 there had also been dialogue between John Hume and Gerry Adams, which attempted to draw Sinn Féin into the political arena. Through its association with the SDLP, Sinn Féin was hoping to establish a broadly based nationalist movement which would have the support of the Dublin government. Furthermore, between October 1990 and November 1993 there were secret contacts between British government officials and leading Sinn Féin figures such as Martin McGuinness (1950–), a sign that the British authorities were privately conceding the importance of involving Sinn Féin in political dialogue. Considerable rethinking had also been occurring within the Provisional movement itself, with a growing emphasis being placed on seeking political legitimacy as opposed to a continuation of the armed struggle.

In 1991 Brooke succeeded in getting talks started between all the constitutional parties in Northern Ireland, excluding Sinn Féin. There were three separate strands to these talks: internal relations within Northern Ireland; arrangements between Northern Ireland and the Dublin government; and relations between London and Dublin. These talks continued until November 1992 under a new Northern Ireland secretary, Sir Patrick Mayhew. Although they failed to reach agreement on any of the three strands, they had established an agenda for future negotiations where 'nothing would be agreed in any strand until everything is agreed in the talks as a whole'.

Meanwhile, sectarian murders and bombings continued. The steady rise in loyalist paramilitary violence resulted in the random assassination of Catholics, while in April 1992 the IRA exploded a huge bomb at the Baltic Exchange in the centre of London, which killed three people and caused damage amounting to hundreds of millions of pounds. Despite this violence, the secret and overt political activity of the previous years within Northern Ireland, together with the continuing co-operation between the British and Irish governments, were leading to the possibility of dramatic political movement towards an Anglo-Irish peace process.

15

THE POLITICS OF PEACE
1993–1998

The year 1993 witnessed continuing violence by republican and loyalist paramilitaries in Northern Ireland,
and frequent IRA attacks in Britain. In March an IRA
explosion in Warrington, Cheshire, resulted in the deaths of
two young boys and provoked widespread public revulsion
in Britain and both parts of Ireland, though many in Northern
Ireland had long since grown accustomed to such tragedies. The
following month a huge IRA bomb exploded in Bishopsgate,
the heart of London's financial district, killing one person and
causing damage estimated at over £1,000 million.

Despite this sustained violence, significant political developments were taking place behind the scenes. Confidential
talks began in April 1993 between John Hume and Gerry
Adams in an attempt to find common ground on a political
settlement. Since the early 1980s the Catholic vote in Northern Ireland had been split between the SDLP and Sinn Féin.

Both parties had considerable electoral support, although the SDLP preponderated, and by now Sinn Féin had lost its only seat at Westminster. Hume was attempting to persuade Sinn Féin to use its popular electoral mandate to reject violence and enter the political process, and stressed the significance of the 1990 declaration by the then Northern Ireland secretary, Peter Brooke, that Great Britain had no 'selfish strategic or economic interest in Northern Ireland'. Although Hume was heavily criticised by many on both sides of the water for 'talking to terrorists', he refused to be diverted from his efforts to bring about an end to IRA violence and create a peace process.

The positive response of Taoiseach Albert Reynolds to the Hume–Adams talks infuriated unionists and loyalist paramilitaries. The latter declared their intention to increase their attacks on the nationalist community whose representatives, they alleged, were participating in a pan-nationalist front comprising the SDLP, IRA, Sinn Féin and the southern government in order to negotiate over the heads of the unionist people. The spiral of violence culminated in one particularly blood-drenched week in October 1993 when twenty-four people met violent deaths, including nine innocent civilians who died as a result of an IRA bomb in a fish shop on the Protestant Shankill Road in Belfast. The UFF quickly retaliated with an attack on a public house in Greysteel, County Londonderry, in which seven people died.

In November 1993 it was revealed that, despite earlier denials, the British government had been having secret talks with leading Sinn Féin spokesman, Martin McGuinness, for three years. This news greatly increased unionist fears of a sell-out and complicated the government's precarious parliamentary position. Prime Minister John Major had emerged from the 1992 general election with a much diminished majority, and his government's controversial policy towards the European Union made it increasingly dependent on the votes of unionists to maintain its authority. Indeed, it was these votes which saved the government from defeat during the debate on the Maastricht treaty in July 1993.

It was important, therefore, for both the British and Irish governments to win back the initiative from the Hume–Adams negotiations, and from both sets of paramilitaries. Eventually, on 15 December 1993, the two premiers, Major and Reynolds, issued a Joint Declaration on Northern Ireland at 10 Downing Street. This was a complex and finely balanced document which was effectively aimed at bringing Sinn Féin into the realm of constitutional politics. It accepted that a united Ireland could be achieved by constitutional means, though only with the consent of the majority in Northern Ireland. It also signalled that Britain was willing to end the Union if a northern majority wished it, and reiterated that the government had no 'selfish strategic or economic interest in Northern Ireland'. In addition, it offered Sinn Féin an opportunity to engage in peace talks, provided the IRA ended its violent campaign.

While most of the constitutional political parties in Northern Ireland, with the exception of Ian Paisley's DUP, accepted the document as a basis for future political dialogue, Sinn Féin remained hesitant. The declaration placed the party in a difficult position. It had been offered a possible entry into talks, yet there was no indication in the document of an early British withdrawal from Northern Ireland. However, if the violence continued, much of the blame would be placed upon the IRA. Sinn Féin did not reject the declaration outright, therefore, but instead sought 'clarification' from the government on a number of issues in order to buy time. Meanwhile, the bloody cycle of violence continued. In March 1994 the IRA launched a mortar attack at London's Heathrow Airport, and in June UVF gunmen attacked a public house in Loughinisland, County Down, where customers were watching a World Cup football match, and killed six people in retaliation for earlier republican killings.

By now, however, the Sinn Féin leadership had been redefining its political strategy and had established close dialogue with Taoiseach Reynolds and the Dublin government. This was reinforced by new links with the United States, where there was an important Irish-American lobby of politicians and businessmen influencing American policy on Northern Ireland at the highest level. They managed to persuade the Clinton administration that granting a visa to Gerry Adams to visit the United States would strengthen his support for a democratic peace process within his own movement and so take the gun out of republican politics. The British government was strenuously opposed to granting Adams a visa, not least because it would enable him to gain much needed publicity for his cause in America. President Clinton rejected this opposition, however, and the Sinn Féin leader arrived in America on 31 January 1994 to address a conference hosted by the National Committee on American Foreign Policy, emerging from the obscurity of domestic broadcasting bans into a blaze of international media attention.

The price of this Irish and American governmental goodwill was that, if Adams was to be accepted as a genuine peacemaker, and the republican movement to be allowed political influence in a talks process, there had to be a commitment to wholly peaceful methods from Sinn Féin and the IRA. Thus, after a long process of consultation and debate, the whole republican military strategy was reassessed, and its supporters required to adopt a 'totally unarmed strategy' in order to achieve a negotiated political settlement. The result came on 31 August

1994 when the IRA announced 'a complete cessation of military operations' which was greeted triumphantly in nationalist areas, but also with relief elsewhere in Northern Ireland, however stunned and sceptical people were.

Six weeks later, on 13 October, after an internal consultative process, the loyalist paramilitary groups, under the umbrella of the Combined Loyalist Military Command, announced a similar cessation 'dependent upon the continued cessation of all nationalist/republican violence'. Significantly, the loyalists went further by offering 'to the loved ones of all innocent victims... abject and true remorse'. For the first time in twenty-five years, there was peace. The people of Northern Ireland hardly dared believe that the long nightmare was, in fact, finally over.

The republican cease-fire came about as a result of significant shifts in the position of the Provisional movement and of the British government. Sinn Féin was coming to accept that Britain had indeed little interest in maintaining a foothold in Ireland. The movement also recognised that it would now have to operate its democratic mandate within a loose nationalist coalition involving the SDLP and the southern government, as well as deal with an influential American administration. Similarly, the British government had come to accept the unpalatable fact that the IRA could not be completely defeated in military terms and that Sinn Féin needed to be brought into any effective peace process. It had also accepted the view that the Irish government would have a central role to play in a peace process, and that any long-term settlement would have to include a southern dimension.

The Irish government warmly welcomed the IRA cease-fire declaration and within a week Taoiseach Reynolds, who had played a key role in creating the conditions which led to the cessation, invited John Hume and Gerry Adams to Dublin.

The public handshake between the three leaders in front of the Irish parliament on 6 September was graphic confirmation of the emergence of a new pan-nationalist front comprising the Dublin government, the SDLP and Sinn Féin, which so alarmed Ulster unionists. In sharp contrast, the British government, under pressure in parliament from Tory backbenchers and unionists, reacted most cautiously and demanded assurances that the IRA's cessation was 'permanent'. Much time was lost in arguments over this issue of permanence, and the position was further complicated when the British insisted that the IRA would have to decommission some of its arms 'as a tangible confidence-building measure' before Sinn Féin could be admitted to all-party talks. This insistence on partial decommissioning led to serious disagreements between the Irish and British governments in the autumn of 1994, since Dublin believed that this precondition was hindering real progress in the peace talks.

From a British perspective, disarming the enemy through a decommissioning process would ease the problem of dealing with the IRA by weakening its ability to engage in military activity. Sinn Féin, however, warned that this was a new and unacceptable precondition which, if insisted upon, would threaten the whole peace initiative. It claimed that the government, having failed to defeat the IRA militarily, was now trying to defeat it through peace talks. It argued that decommissioning was tantamount to surrender, leaving nationalist communities at the mercy of arms held by the Protestant community and by the police and army, whom they could not trust. Many nationalists questioned the motives of the British government and became suspicious of the consequences of Major's increasing dependency upon the unionists at Westminster to sustain his government. Others came to doubt the practicalities of decommissioning and the difficulties of verifying that it had in fact taken place. Nevertheless, for over a year the British government insisted that some agreement on arms decommissioning had to be in place before all-party talks could begin.

Meanwhile, the two governments attempted to move forward the political initiative on 22 February 1995 by issuing the Frameworks Documents, which set out their views on how a permanent peace settlement might be reached. Although it stressed that Northern Ireland would remain part of the United Kingdom as long as a majority of its population so desired, unionists were greatly alarmed, and nationalists heartened, by the proposal to set up a joint north–south body with executive powers over certain issues. While the British government tried to represent itself as a neutral facilitator, saying that the document offered something for everyone, unionists claimed that John Major was now operating according to a nationalist agenda.

The imminent arrival of President Clinton on an official visit to Ireland at the end of November 1995 led to frantic last-minute diplomatic activity in Dublin and London to resolve the decommissioning issue. A twin-track strategy was announced, aimed at achieving all-party talks by February 1996, and at the same time setting up an international body to report on arms decommissioning, chaired by former US Senator George Mitchell. It was a useful fudge, which enabled Clinton to throw his support behind it, and thus make it more difficult for Sinn Féin to reject. Clinton's visit to Northern Ireland, the first ever by a US president, was a triumphant one. He was warmly welcomed by almost all shades of opinion, and seemed to have revitalised the peace process, as well as revealing how much the Northern Ireland question had now become internationalised. With an American presidential election due to take place within a year, Clinton was conscious that

Ireland was one of his few foreign policy successes. Cynics, however, suggested that the real motive behind his trip was his desire to win the support of the estimated forty million Americans who claimed Irish ancestry.

John Major's government had by now lost its overall majority in the Commons and was even more dependent for survival on the votes of the nine Ulster Unionist MPs, now led by David Trimble (1944–), and the three Democratic Unionists. When the Mitchell report was published on 24 January 1996 it stated that there was no prospect of the IRA decommissioning its weapons before all-party talks took place, and recommended that this should occur during, rather than before, political negotiations. However, Major effectively ignored Mitchell's key proposals by announcing that there would be elections for a new Northern Ireland assembly before all-party talks could begin. The fact that this idea had earlier been proposed by the unionists led John Hume to accuse Major and his government of trying 'to buy votes to keep themselves in power'.

The lack of movement towards all-party negotiations over the previous eighteen months, coupled with the government's response to the Mitchell report, caused much dismay in republican ranks and brought to the surface the many tensions within the IRA military command. The tragic result was the ending of the IRA cease-fire on 9 February 1996, when a massive bomb exploded at Canary Wharf in London, killing two people and causing damage estimated at over £80 million. The IRA blamed the collapse of the cease-fire on the British government's refusal to set up all-party talks until paramilitary arms had been decommissioned, and on what it saw as Major's sidelining of the Mitchell report. These criticisms were vehemently rejected by government ministers, who instead blamed the breakdown on Sinn Féin's refusal to yield on the decommissioning issue. To many people in Ireland, and to some in Britain, the refusal of Major's government to enter fully into negotiations with Sinn Féin representatives on the basis of their links with the IRA was unconvincing. Similar conflicts in other parts of the world had been resolved by negotiations involving all parties and groups, irrespective of their previous associations. Some observers, moreover, suggested that Adams, who had played a crucial role in persuading the IRA to abandon violence, had ultimately been let down by the organisation's decision to resume its military campaign and that his influence over the Provisionals was waning. More realistic analysts, however, understood that it was always going to be difficult for Adams to condemn the IRA in public, and that he would be a key figure if the cease-fire was to be restored in the future.

Strenuous efforts were made to try to resurrect the peace process and to maintain the Dublin–London accord, despite disquiet in Dublin at British government policy on decommissioning and the proposed new assembly. At the end of February a firm date, 10 June, was set for all-party talks to begin, and elections to the negotiating forum took place in May. The result provided little comfort for the government, with Sinn Féin winning seventeen seats and over 15 per cent of the vote. This was the party's best electoral performance to date, and its advances were made mainly at the expense of the SDLP, which won twenty-one seats and over 21 per cent of the vote.

When the talks eventually began in June 1996 under the chairmanship of George Mitchell, Sinn Féin was refused entry until the IRA declared an unconditional cessation of violence. A renewal of the republican cease-fire seemed as far away as ever when the Provisionals exploded a one-and-a-half-ton bomb in the centre of Manchester on 15 June, injuring two hundred people and causing enormous damage. However, in practice, the IRA cease-fire continued in Northern Ireland, as did the loyalist cessation. Nevertheless, great damage was done to community relations during the summer months, the traditional marching season of the Protestant Orange Order. The most crucial incident occurred when the RUC decided to reroute an Orange parade from Drumcree church in Portadown, County Armagh, away from the Catholic Garvaghy Road.

The original plan to march along the Garvaghy Road, an area which had once been mainly Protestant but was now predominantly Catholic, was seen as provocative by the residents. Unionists, however, viewed the police decision to re-route the march through a mainly Protestant area as an act of appeasement to nationalists. This led to four days of loyalist rioting throughout Northern Ireland until the RUC eventually capitulated on 11 July and allowed the Orange march to proceed along the Garvaghy Road. This in turn led to rioting in republican areas, and a continuing series of sectarian attacks on churches, individuals and private property. This violent conflict with the RUC led many in the nationalist community to repeat their traditional accusation that this overwhelmingly Protestant police force was again failing to be impartial in its policing. Thus, the whole Drumcree episode served to poison community relations, and led even moderate Catholics to call for the disbandment of the force. The RUC defended its actions by claiming that it was in an invidious, no-win situation, caught between two equally uncompromising opponents. Cardinal Cahal Daly expressed anger at the reversal of the RUC's decision, claiming to have been 'personally betrayed by the British government', while Fine Gael leader, John Bruton, called it a 'mistake'. The whole question of the routing of marches remains a deeply sensitive one, and in recent years it has become an annual barometer of the level of mutual hostility which exists between the two communities in Northern Ireland.

The outlook for the peace process at the end of 1996 was bleak. The IRA cease-fire was over and Sinn Féin remained excluded from political talks. To make matters worse, the British government's ability and willingness to manoeuvre at Westminster was greatly hampered by its dependence on the unionists for its overall parliamentary majority. Meanwhile, Hume and Adams were attempting to broker a resumption of the cease-fire in order to help Sinn Féin gain unconditional entry to the talks process, for which they sought a definite time frame. Major's increasingly weak Conservative government was eventually defeated in the British general election in May 1997, which resulted in a large Labour majority of 179 seats. In Northern Ireland Gerry Adams and Martin McGuinness both won seats, one from the DUP, the other from the SDLP. These gains were seen as a vindication of the party's non-violent strategy and strengthened its demands to be admitted to all-party talks on the basis of its democratic mandate. The Ulster Unionists won 10 seats, with the SDLP, DUP and UK Unionists returning 3, 2 and 1 MPs respectively. The following month saw the fall of the Bruton administration in the Republic and the formation of a new coalition government under Fianna Fáil's Bertie Ahern (1951–). Thus, in both Britain and Ireland, a fresh approach to the problems of Northern Ireland appeared possible.

Both governments immediately stressed the importance of restoring momentum to the peace process. Prime Minister Tony Blair (1953–) offered Sinn Féin entry to the talks if an unconditional IRA cease-fire was restored and Taoiseach Ahern adopted a more pro-nationalist approach to the process than his predecessor. The British government's large parliamentary majority meant that unionist votes were now of little significance, in contrast with the pre-election situation. This fresh governmental commitment to pursue an energetic joint strategy was soon confronted by familiar obstacles, however. The killing of two policemen in Lurgan, County Armagh, by the IRA in June, and the unyielding determination of Orangemen to march along their 'traditional' Drumcree route in July meant that, on the surface at least, the summer of 1997 offered little hope for the people of Northern Ireland.

The Drumcree march proved to be a crucial flashpoint yet again. The new Northern Ireland secretary, Marjorie (Mo) Mowlam (1949–), who was well liked and respected, spent some months trying to reach a compromise solution between Orange marchers and Catholic residents. Having failed to achieve this, she made a last-minute decision to allow the march to proceed along the Garvaghy Road. She stated that she did this on the recommendation of her security advisers, in particular the RUC chief constable, Ronnie Flanagan, who spoke of there being 'a simple stark choice between two evils'. This decision, which was publicly criticised by the Dublin government, outraged nationalists and led to serious rioting throughout Northern Ireland. There was real danger of a major escalation of violence during the Orange marches of 12 July; however, a few days beforehand, Orangemen took the dramatic decision to call off some crucial marches which would have passed through Catholic areas, including the lower Ormeau Road in Belfast.

This conciliatory decision, which was bitterly criticised by some hardline Orangemen, brought about a remarkable lessening of political tension and the marches of 12 July took place peacefully. Northern Ireland had once again pulled back from the precipice of civil war, and the concessions made by the Orange Order led to the republican movement coming under increased pressure from the Irish and British governments, as well as the Clinton administration, to renew the IRA cease-fire. A response came remarkably quickly on 19 July, when the IRA declared a new cease-fire to take effect from the next day. Although the thorny question of arms decommissioning remained unresolved, Prime Minister Blair rapidly seized the opportunity provided by the cessation to agree that Sinn Féin should be admitted to all-party talks after a short six-week period to test whether violence had really ended. At the end of August Blair accepted that the IRA cease-fire was genuine, and in September Sinn Féin signed up to the Mitchell principles, which committed it to using exclusively peaceful means to resolve political disputes. A few days before the talks were due to begin, however, the IRA stated that it had difficulty with some of the Mitchell principles, and also that it would not hand over weapons. The timing of this statement put pressure on the Sinn Féin leadership, which now attempted to distance itself from the IRA, emphasising that the party had a political mandate to be present at the talks as a result of its recent strong showing in local and national elections.

Despite this setback, the talks began as scheduled on 15 September 1997 at Stormont Castle. At first the various unionist parties refused to sit at the same negotiating table as Sinn Féin, but eventually they did so, with the exception of Paisley's DUP and Robert McCartney's marginal UK Unionist Party. The two small unionist parties associated with loyalist paramilitaries, the Progressive Unionist Party and the Ulster Democratic Party, were an integral element in the negotiations. Inevitably there was little sign of progress in the early weeks and much political posturing took place, but at least after many years of frustrated effort and false hope, the different political groupings in Northern Ireland were in the same room together and talking.

A deadline for the conclusion of the talks had been set

for May 1998, but by the end of 1997 there had been little substantial progress, and much time was taken up with endless procedural disputes. In October Blair visited Belfast in an effort to inject new impetus into the peace process. There he met and shook hands with Gerry Adams, the encounter deliberately taking place behind closed doors, away from prying camera lens. It was a bold move by Blair, and one which Major had always refused when in office. The handshake was both historic and symbolic, as it was the first time a British prime minister had formally met with a Sinn Féin leader since Lloyd George had done so in 1921. While nationalists welcomed the prime minister's initiative, Conservatives and unionists criticised him for what they saw as yet another concession to republican demands for recognition.

For Blair, the political danger of the meeting was outweighed by the prospect of confirming Sinn Féin's commitment to constitutional politics. For Adams, the risk of alienating his militant republican support was counterbalanced by the official acceptance of his party as a legitimate element of the peace negotiations. The Sinn Féin leader was nevertheless taking a calculated political gamble, as divisions were now evident within the republican movement. The breakaway Continuity IRA had earlier condemned the whole process and some new defections had appeared in Sinn Féin ranks. In a further attempt to bind the republican movement into the talks process, Blair invited the Sinn Féin leadership to Downing Street on 11 December. This was another historically resonant meeting, as the last time such an event occurred was in December 1921 when Michael Collins and Arthur Griffith led the Sinn Féin delegation to London to negotiate the Anglo-Irish Treaty.

Later in December, however, the whole peace process was thrown into crisis by the assassination of the leader of the Loyalist Volunteer Force, Billy Wright, in the Maze prison by members of the republican Irish National Liberation Army, and the killing of a number of innocent Catholics by the LVF and the Ulster Freedom Fighters in retaliation. The threat of loyalist paramilitary prisoners to withdraw their support for the talks process led Ulster Unionist leader, David Trimble, to visit them in order to exchange views on the progress of the negotiations. The meeting highlighted the uneasy relationship between mainstream unionism and loyalist extremism, and Trimble, having spoken directly to some of the most hardened gunmen in Northern Ireland, would find it difficult in the future to refuse similar discussions with republican leaders.

A few days later Mo Mowlam made a dramatic and unprecedented visit to the Maze also, where she too had face-to-face meetings with these loyalist leaders. Although her efforts to maintain the vital loyalist prisoner support for the talks process proved successful, the admission by the UFF that it had murdered three Catholics led to the four-week withdrawal of its political representatives, the Ulster Democratic Party, from the talks on 26 January, before they could be expelled for violating the Mitchell principles. This development deepened anxieties that the peace process was on the verge of collapse, and that sectarian violence was about to return to the streets of Northern Ireland.

Despite these setbacks, the two governments urgently attempted to push the process forward by publishing outline proposals for a joint north–south body and a new Council of the Isles which would include England, Scotland and Wales, as well as both parts of Ireland. These proposals were an attempt to offer concessions to both sides, but the crucial question of the powers of these new bodies remained undefined. A new hurdle emerged on 20 February, when both governments reluctantly excluded Sinn Féin from the talks process for a two-week period, despite protests from the republican leadership. This move was prompted by RUC reports of the IRA's involvement in two recent killings, which, if true, constituted a violation of the Mitchell principles. The explosion of a large car bomb in Moira, County Down, later that evening threatened a return to more sustained violence, even though it was alleged that this was the work of the Continuity IRA rather than the IRA.

These combined setbacks to the peace negotiations led some to conclude that the whole process had become fatally flawed, and that the temporary exclusions were creating a farcical scenario. Certainly much had changed within a year, with principles such as the refusal to 'talk to terrorists' and the insistence that arms be decommissioned before talks begin being quietly dropped. Nevertheless, both governments remained committed to presenting a political settlement for approval by referendum to the people of both parts of Ireland by mid-1998. The search for a settlement acquired fresh urgency in March, following chairman George Mitchell's announcement of 9 April as the official deadline for the conclusion of the talks process. Negotiations became more intensive in the weeks leading up to this date and the political drama deepened as the deadline approached.

With two days of negotiations left, all-party agreement seemed as far away as ever, as unionists and nationalists remained locked in stalemate over two key elements of a political agreement: the powers and structure of a Northern Ireland assembly and a north–south ministerial council. With the fearful prospect of the talks being about to collapse, chairman Mitchell produced a draft document which unionists immediately denounced as 'a Sinn Féin wish-list'. On the night of Tuesday 7 April Prime Minister Blair arrived in Belfast, where he was later joined by Taoiseach Ahern, in an attempt to resolve these centrally divisive issues. For the next three days the two leaders and the Northern Ireland political parties were locked in intensive, round-the-clock negotiating sessions in Castle Buildings at Stormont, closely monitored from without by an anxious public and expectant world media. News that a historic agreement had been reached eventually came on the afternoon of Good Friday, 10 April, when chairman Mitchell announced that the two governments and the Northern Ireland parties had arrived at a landmark political settlement.

The deal proposed the establishment of a 108-member Northern Ireland assembly with executive and legislative powers, elected by proportional representation and run by a committee of 12 ministers. Key decisions taken by the assembly would require the assent of a majority from both communities, thereby invoking the principle of 'parallel consent'. The first duty of this assembly would be to set up a north–south ministerial council, accountable to the assembly and to the Irish parliament. This body, representative of those with executive authority in Belfast and Dublin, would meet to exchange information and deal with matters of cross-border co-operation. In order to facilitate these new institutional arrangements, the Irish government proposed to amend Articles 2 and 3 of its constitution, which lay claim to the territory of Northern Ireland, while its British counterpart pledged itself to repeal the 1920 Government of Ireland Act, thereby relinquishing the supreme authority of Westminster over Northern Ireland. A further proposal for the establishment of a British–Irish Council, with members drawn from both parts of Ireland, Westminster and the new Scottish and Welsh assemblies, was also agreed upon. Additional articles proposed the establishment of an independent commission to make recommendations about a new police structure for Northern Ireland, and made provision for the release within two years of all prisoners linked to paramilitary organisations which were on cease-fire.

Despite opposition from dissidents within republican and unionist ranks, the agreement received a muted but positive welcome from most sections of Irish, British and international opinion. Indeed, the coincidence of the potentially epoch-making agreement with the religious festival of Easter encouraged many to hope that the Christian message of forgiveness and reconciliation might at last be heeded by both communities in Northern Ireland. Such sentiments were most eloquently expressed by Ireland's Nobel laureate, Seamus Heaney, who saw in the agreement the potential for a lasting peace and shared future for all the people of Ireland:

> If revolution is the kicking down of a rotten door, evolution is more like pushing the stone from the mouth of the tomb. There is an Easter energy about it, a sense of arrival rather than wreckage, and what is nonpareil about the new conditions is the promise they offer of a new covenant between people living in this island of Ireland. For once, and at long last, the language of the Bible can be appropriated by those with a vision of the future rather than those who sing the battle hymns of the past.

The first crucial test came six weeks later on 22 May, when simultaneous referendums on the Easter settlement took place in both parts of Ireland. An overwhelming 94 per cent of those who voted in the Republic supported the agreement, while a substantial 71 per cent of northern voters also endorsed it. This outcome represented the most significant political decision of the Irish people since the 1921 treaty, yet it was clear to everyone that hopes of a lasting settlement were still threatened by political opponents and men of violence on both sides. Although a large majority of Sinn Féin delegates had backed the agreement at their *ard fheis* (annual conference) in April, not all members of the Provisional movement supported the political strategy being pursued. Indeed some dissident IRA members remained committed to a continuation of the armed struggle and were in the process of setting up a new organisation which would enable them to continue it. Unionists were also divided on the agreement. Although David Trimble managed, with difficulty, to secure his party's support for the accord, there was determined opposition from the DUP, most members of the Orange Order and dissident loyalist paramilitaries, as well as from some of his own party colleagues.

Meanwhile, the British government, mindful of the obstacles to the implementation of the agreement, attempted to bolster public confidence in the north by announcing details of a major £60 million investment project to establish a cross-community university on the peace line dividing Protestant and Catholic areas of west Belfast, as well as offering a financial aid package to boost the economy. It was in an atmosphere of cautious optimism tinged with apprehension, therefore, that elections for the Northern Ireland assembly took place on 26 June. Although the turn-out of 70 per cent was significantly down on the previous month's referendum, the great majority of voters supported pro-agreement parties. The final result was: Ulster Unionist Party, 28; SDLP, 24; DUP, 20; Sinn Féin, 18; Alliance Party, 6; UK Unionist Party, 5; Northern Ireland Women's Coalition, 2; Progressive Unionist Party, 2; Independent Unionists, 3.

This outcome highlighted the serious divisions within unionism regarding the Good Friday Agreement. The Ulster Unionist Party, and in particular its leader, Trimble, barely managed to secure a majority of unionist votes, and suffered something of a psychological blow in having its worst election result in many years, being overtaken for the first time by the

SDLP as the party which secured the most first preference votes. Meanwhile, Sinn Féin recorded its highest ever vote, receiving over 17 per cent of first preferences. This meant that Trimble was now highly vulnerable to criticism from anti-agreement opponents within his own party, as well as being open to attacks from without by Paisley's DUP and McCartney's UK Unionists. Unionist divisions were clearly in evidence during the inaugural meeting of the Northern Ireland assembly on 1 July, at which Trimble was elected First Minister designate, with the SDLP's Seamus Mallon (1936–) as his deputy. Among pro-agreement unionists, the most sensitive issue was the prospect of their representatives having to sit in a power-sharing executive with members of Sinn Féin, whose electoral strength entitled them to two ministerial positions. Trimble's supporters made it clear to him that before this could happen, he must secure the decommissioning of IRA weapons and a declaration from Sinn Féin that the war was over. Otherwise, their support for him – and for the agreement – would be in jeopardy.

The decommissioning issue, which first arose in 1994, was soon to grow into a major obstacle, but in the aftermath of the elections the most immediate problem for both governments was the renewed controversy surrounding the annual Drumcree Orange parade scheduled for 6 July, which in previous years had been the cause of so much sectarian tension and violence. On 29 June the recently established Independent Parades Commission banned Orangemen from marching on their traditional route from Drumcree church along the Garvaghy Road into Portadown. The decision was rejected by the Orange Order's eighty thousand members, most of whom were opposed to the Good Friday deal, which they regarded as the latest and most damaging in a series of political sell-outs. To them, the ban represented a further erosion of their civil and cultural rights. They were determined to defy it; Drumcree would be their last stand.

Tension mounted as the day of the march approached. From 4 July onwards, hundreds of soldiers, assisted by RUC officers, dug themselves in behind a deep trench and erected concrete barriers to block the planned route of the assembled marchers, whose numbers had swollen to twenty-five thousand by 10 July. The situation soon deteriorated into violence, with petrol bombs and blast bombs being thrown at the security forces by angry Orangemen. Violent sectarian clashes followed throughout Northern Ireland. Families were driven from their homes, shops and businesses were attacked and Catholic churches burned. With Orangemen threatening to bring a further eighty thousand loyalists to Drumcree during the annual 12 July parades, it looked as though the north was once again about to topple over into the abyss of destruction. The Drumcree stand-off had effectively become a trial of strength between those who wished to sabotage the agreement and those who wanted it to succeed.

However, popular Protestant opinion began to ebb away from the Orange extremists as their violence against the security forces sickened many supporters. The defining moment of the crisis came in the early hours of 12 July, when a loyalist petrol-bomb attack on a house in Ballymoney, County Antrim, resulted in the horrific deaths by fire of three young brothers, aged seven, nine and ten. The widespread revulsion provoked by the deaths of these innocent boys turned public opinion decidedly against the marchers and prompted many appeals from political and religious leaders for the 'siege of Drumcree' to be lifted. With the Orange Order now deeply divided, the protesters began to leave Drumcree in their thousands, leaving a small number of hardline demonstrators to maintain a token protest. Although it had come perilously close to destruction, the agreement had survived its first serious test. Within weeks, however, it was to be tested again.

Hopes that the lessons of Drumcree would end violence for good in Northern Ireland were summarily and tragically shattered on 15 August when the Real IRA, a republican splinter group opposed to the Good Friday settlement, detonated a massive car bomb in Omagh, County Tyrone. A misleading warning was given, but the bomb exploded in a crowded shopping area, killing twenty-nine people as a result and injuring over two hundred others. The bombing was the bloodiest single atrocity of the Troubles and united everyone on the island in shock, grief and outrage. One of the most striking responses came from Gerry Adams, whose public condemnation of a republican act of violence was unprecedented. The reaction of the dissidents themselves was significant also. Confronted by a deepening mood of public anger and hostility, particularly from within their own republican constituency, the Real IRA quickly announced a suspension of its military operations and soon declared a complete cease-fire. The INLA's decision to call a cessation, also, left only one republican paramilitary grouping, the Continuity IRA, not on cease-fire.

The Omagh atrocity strengthened the resolve of both governments and most northern politicians to continue to work towards the implementation of the peace settlement. Both the Irish and British parliaments were recalled from their summer recesses in the wake of the tragedy to enact draconian emergency counter-terrorist legislation aimed at crushing any remaining paramilitary opposition to the Good Friday accord. Among the provisions of the new laws were restrictions on a suspect's right to silence, increased powers of detention and the right of the state to seize property used for the storage of weapons. While public reaction to these harsh security measures was muted, some civil rights groups criticised the lack of adequate prior scrutiny and consultation, and expressed concern about the threat to human rights posed by the new legislation.

Despite their criticisms of the hasty actions of the Irish and British legislatures in the wake of the Omagh bombing, Sinn Féin's continued support for the agreement was underlined by Adams's statement of 1 September that 'the violence we have seen must be for all of us now a thing of the past, over, done with and gone'. This was widely interpreted as a tacit admission by the republican movement that the IRA cease-fire was indeed permanent and that there would be no return to violence. A few days later, President Clinton made his second visit to Northern Ireland and the Republic in three years, and pledged additional moral and financial support for the settlement. Further international endorsement came in October, when John Hume and David Trimble were jointly awarded the Nobel peace prize for their courageous contribution to the peace process. While people in both parts of Ireland rejoiced at the news, their delight was tempered by the recognition that significant barriers to a lasting political settlement remained.

As 1998 drew to a close, it was clear that the issue of arms decommissioning had once again become a major stumbling block to progress. Although leading Sinn Féin negotiator Martin McGuinness had been appointed to establish liaison with the decommissioning body in September, the IRA still refused to hand over any of its weapons or explosives. This increased First Minister Trimble's difficulties with recalcitrant unionists and led to his refusal to appoint a shadow power-sharing executive, which would include Sinn Féin representatives, or move towards the establishment of north–south bodies as specified by the agreement. Sinn Féin responded by claiming that it was entitled to seats on the executive on the basis of its electoral mandate, and that Trimble's demand was an unacceptable precondition not included in the Good Friday Agreement, which states only that parties must use their influence to ensure decommissioning is completed within two years. Neither Trimble nor Adams were free agents, however, and both were aware of splits within their own parties. A political stalemate soon developed, and the key 31 October deadline for the announcement of the shadow executive and the setting up of cross-border institutions passed without agreement being reached. The sectarian killing of a Catholic man in Belfast by a renegade loyalist paramilitary group, the Red Hand Defenders, on that same date acted as a dreadful reminder to all parties of the potential consequences of political failure.

While the serious impasse over decommissioning remained, other aspects of the Good Friday Agreement had been successfully implemented. A considerable number of paramilitary prisoners from both communities had been released and an Independent Commission on Policing to examine the role of the RUC was operating under the chairmanship of former Hong Kong governor, Chris Patten. The prospects for a successful settlement in Northern Ireland were further underpinned by the growing maturity and warmth of the relationship between Britain and the Republic of Ireland. This closeness was symbolised by the Armistice Day meeting of President McAleese and Queen Elizabeth, who jointly inaugurated a peace memorial near Ypres in Belgium, where Irish unionist and nationalist soldiers fought side by side for the only time in the First World War, during the early stages of the Battle of Passchendaele. This historic occasion marked the first official recognition by the Irish Republic of the tens of thousands of Irishmen who fought and died for the Allied cause in the war.

History was again made later in November, when Tony Blair became the first British prime minister to address both houses of the Irish parliament. While he acknowledged that the peace process was at a difficult juncture, he also observed that Northern Ireland, which had divided the two countries for so long, was now bringing Ireland and Britain closer together.

Significant signs of political progress soon followed. On 18 December unionist and nationalist leaders reached agreement on the shape of a new Northern Ireland administration, comprising ten departments to be operated jointly by representatives from both sides of the political divide. They also agreed on issues of north–south co-operation and implementation, as stipulated in the Good Friday Agreement. The proposed establishment of six cross-border bodies was announced, to deal with such matters as trade and business development, marine affairs and the promotion of the Irish and Ulster Scots languages. These hopeful developments were further reinforced on the same day when the LVF became the first paramilitary group to decommission its weapons by handing over a small quantity of guns and explosives to the decommissioning body.

It is too soon to say yet whether this progress will continue, or where it will end. All realise that the road to peace and reconciliation will be a long and arduous one, with many obstacles yet to be negotiated before what Blair called 'the burden of history' can finally be lifted from the shoulders of the Irish and British people. Meanwhile, Northern Ireland remains poised between the hope of new beginnings and the despair of old hatreds. The emergence of a new and just society will ultimately depend upon the ingenuity, goodwill and spirit of compromise of its people and their leaders. Perhaps, after centuries of conflict, violence and bloodshed, the Irish and British nations are about to arrive at that longed-for, elusive moment when, in the words of Seamus Heaney, 'hope and history rhyme'.

CHRONOLOGY
1690–1998

1690

JUNE William of Orange arrives in Ireland.

JULY Williamite army defeats the army of James II at the Battle of the Boyne; James flees to France.

SEPTEMBER William returns to England having failed to capture Limerick.

1691

JULY Williamites defeat Jacobites at the Battle of Aughrim, County Galway.

OCTOBER Treaty of Limerick; Patrick Sarsfield and the remainder of the Irish Jacobite army sail for France to serve in the armies of Louis XIV.

DECEMBER English Act of Parliament bars Catholics from becoming members of parliament or holding public office in Ireland.

1692

OCTOBER First meeting of William's Irish parliament.

1695

SEPTEMBER Irish parliament passes penal laws restricting rights of Catholics to education, to keep arms or to own a horse worth five pounds or more.

1696

APRIL Import duties removed from Irish linen entering England.

1697

SEPTEMBER Act banishing Catholic bishops and regular clergy from Ireland.

1698

APRIL   William Molyneux's *The Case of Ireland's Being Bound by Act of Parliament in England Stated* published in Dublin.

1699

JANUARY   First of a series of Acts restricting Irish woollen exports.

1702

MARCH   Accession of Queen Anne.

1704

MARCH   Act restricting rights of Catholics to own or lease land and imposing a sacramental test on Catholics and Dissenters wishing to hold public office.

1707

MAY   Act of Union between England and Scotland.

1710

JANUARY   Start of two years of agrarian unrest in Connacht, characterised by the houghing (maiming) of livestock.

1713

JUNE   Jonathan Swift installed as dean of St Patrick's Cathedral, Dublin.

1714

AUGUST   Accession of George I.

1715

SEPTEMBER   Jacobite rising in Scotland.

1719

NOVEMBER   Toleration Act grants educational and religious liberties to Dissenters.

1720

APRIL   Declaratory Act asserts the right of the British parliament to legislate for Ireland.

1722

JULY   Patent granting William Wood exclusive right to mint copper coinage for Ireland provokes hostile reaction from Irish political establishment.

1725

SEPTEMBER   Cancellation of William Wood's patent.

1727

JUNE   Accession of George II.
AUGUST   Start of three years of poor harvests causing widespread famine in Ireland.

1728

MAY   Act depriving Catholics of parliamentary franchise.

1729

OCTOBER   Jonathan Swift's *A Modest Proposal* published anonymously in Dublin.

1731

OCTOBER   Irish parliament meets at Parliament House, College Green, Dublin, for first time.

1739

DECEMBER   Severe winter weather precipitates major famine which lasts until 1741.

1742

APRIL   First performance of Handel's *Messiah* in Dublin.

1745

MAY   Irish brigade helps the French to defeat the British at the Battle of Fontenoy.

1746

APRIL   Defeat of the Jacobite cause at the Battle of Culloden in Scotland.

1752

SEPTEMBER   Gregorian calendar replaces Julian calendar throughout British dominions.

1753

DECEMBER   Money Bill dispute between the Irish parliament and the British government.

1759

NOVEMBER   Henry Flood enters Irish parliament.

1760

OCTOBER   Accession of George III.

1761

OCTOBER   Emergence of the Whiteboy movement in Munster.

1763

JULY   Emergence of the Hearts of Oak movement in Ulster.

1768

FEBRUARY   Octennial Act limits the life of the Irish parliament to eight years.

1771

SEPTEMBER   Benjamin Franklin visits Ireland.

1775

APRIL   Start of American War of Independence.
NOVEMBER   Irish parliament approves the removal of four
thousand troops from Ireland to fight in
America.
DECEMBER   Henry Grattan makes his maiden speech in the
Irish parliament.

1776

JULY   Declaration of American Independence.

1778

MARCH   Formation of first Volunteer company in Belfast.
AUGUST   Catholic Relief Act allows Catholics to lease and
inherit land on the same terms as members of
other religious denominations.

1779

NOVEMBER   Volunteers demonstrate in Dublin in favour of
free trade.

1780

FEBRUARY   British Act allowing Ireland the right to trade
freely with the colonies.
MAY   Relief Act repeals sacramental test, making
Dissenters eligible for public office.

1781

OCTOBER   End of American War of Independence.

1782

FEBRUARY   Dungannon Volunteer convention calls for Irish
legislative independence and a relaxation of the
penal laws.

MAY   Second Catholic Relief Act allows Catholics to own land, except in parliamentary boroughs.

JUNE   Repeal of 1720 Declaratory Act, followed by the amendment of Poynings's Law, gives Irish parliament legislative independence.

JULY   Third Catholic Relief Act allows Catholics to become schoolteachers.

1783

APRIL   British Renunciation Act acknowledges the exclusive right of the Irish parliament to legislate for Ireland.

NOVEMBER   Irish parliament rejects Volunteers' parliamentary Reform Bill.

1784

JULY   Formation of the Protestant Peep o' Day Boys in County Armagh; emergence of Catholic Defender movement in Ulster.

1788

NOVEMBER   Temporary insanity of George III provokes Regency crisis.

1789

JULY   Fall of the Bastille in Paris.

1791

MARCH   Tom Paine's *Rights of Man* published in London.

OCTOBER   Society of United Irishmen founded in Belfast.

NOVEMBER   First meeting of Dublin United Irishmen.

1792

APRIL   Relief Act allows Catholics to practise as lawyers.

JULY   Belfast Harp Festival.

1793

JANUARY   Execution of Louis XVI in Paris.

FEBRUARY   France declares war on Britain.
APRIL   Relief Act grants Catholics the parliamentary
             franchise and certain civil and military
             rights.

1794
MAY   Dublin Society of United Irishmen
             suppressed.

1795
MAY   United Irishmen reconstituted as secret
             oath-bound society.
JUNE   Theobald Wolfe Tone leaves Ireland for
             America
SEPTEMBER   Battle of the Diamond in County Armagh
             leads to the foundation of the Orange
             Order.
OCTOBER   Opening of Catholic seminary at St Patrick's
             College, Maynooth, County Kildare.

1796
FEBRUARY   Tone arrives in France from America.
JULY   First Orange march takes place in Ulster.
SEPTEMBER   Belfast United Irish leaders arrested and charged
             with high treason.
DECEMBER   French fleet under General Lazare Hoche arrives
             in Bantry Bay, County Cork.

1797
MARCH   General Gerard Lake imposes martial law in
             Ulster.

1798
MARCH   Dublin United Irish leaders arrested.
             Martial law imposed.
MAY   United Irishmen rebellion begins in Leinster,
             centring on County Wexford.

JUNE	Rebellion breaks out in counties Antrim and Down led by Henry Joy McCracken and Henry Munro; insurgents defeated at Antrim town and Ballynahinch, County Down. Wexford insurgents defeated by Lake's forces at Vinegar Hill.
AUGUST	French force under General Jean Humbert lands at Killala, County Mayo; his army, reinforced by local peasants, defeats crown forces at Castlebar.
SEPTEMBER	Humbert surrenders to Generals Lake and Cornwallis at Ballinamuck, County Longford.
NOVEMBER	Tone arrested, tried and sentenced to be hanged; commits suicide in prison.

1799

JANUARY	Prime Minister William Pitt makes speech in favour of legislative union of Britain and Ireland in British House of Commons.

1800

MAY	Union Bill introduced in Irish House of Commons.
JUNE	Act of Union receives royal assent.
AUGUST	Last sitting of Irish parliament.

1801

JANUARY	Act of Union takes effect. British and Irish parliaments amalgamated.
FEBRUARY	Pitt resigns as prime minister following conflict with George III over Catholic emancipation; succeeded by Henry Addington.

1803

JULY	Abortive rising by Robert Emmet in Dublin; he was executed in September.

1808

AUGUST   Irish Christian Brothers, a religious teaching
order, founded by Edmund Rice in Waterford.

1815

JUNE   Napoleon defeated at the Battle of Waterloo.

1820

JANUARY   Accession of George IV.

1823

MAY   Foundation of the Catholic Association in
Dublin by Daniel O'Connell.

1824

FEBRUARY   Catholic Association introduces 'Catholic rent'.

1828

JULY   O'Connell elected MP for Clare.

1829

APRIL   Catholic Emancipation Act allows Catholics to
enter parliament and hold civil and military
offices.

1830

FEBRUARY   O'Connell takes seat in House of Commons.
JUNE   Accession of William IV.

1831

SEPTEMBER   Government grants £30,000 to provide for a
national system of elementary education in
Ireland.

1832

AUGUST   Irish Reform Act increases Irish representation
in the House of Commons from 100 to 105 seats
and abolishes 'rotten boroughs'.

1834

APRIL   O'Connell introduces Commons motion on repeal of the Union.

1835

FEBRUARY   Compact between O'Connellites, Whigs and Radicals agreed at Lichfield House, London.

1837

JUNE   Accession of Queen Victoria.

1838

JULY   Poor Relief (Ireland) Act extends some features of the English poor law to Ireland.

1840

APRIL   O'Connell forms Repeal Association.

1841

JUNE   Census: population of Ireland, 8,175,124.

1842

OCTOBER   First issue of the *Nation*, weekly organ of the Young Ireland movement.

1843

AUGUST   O'Connell addresses an estimated crowd of 750,000 at monster repeal meeting at the Hill of Tara, County Meath.

OCTOBER   Government prohibition of monster meeting planned for Clontarf, County Dublin, leads to cancellation of meeting by O'Connell.

1844

MAY   O'Connell fined and sentenced to twelve months' imprisonment; William Smith O'Brien assumes leadership of repeal movement in O'Connell's absence.

SEPTEMBER   O'Connell released from prison following
              reversal of judgment against him by the House
              of Lords.

1845

JUNE   Maynooth College Act greatly increases annual
              grant to the college.
JULY   Colleges (Ireland) Act establishes universities in
              Belfast, Cork and Galway.
SEPTEMBER   First reports of potato blight in Ireland.
NOVEMBER   Prime Minister Sir Robert Peel authorises the
              importation of Indian corn (maize) from
              America.

1846

MARCH   Public Works (Ireland) Act authorises the setting
              up of state-aided relief works to ameliorate
              famine distress.
JUNE   Repeal of the Corn Laws.
              Lord John Russell succeeds Sir Robert Peel
              as prime minister.
JULY   O'Connellites and Young Irelanders split over
              principle of physical force.
AUGUST–
SEPTEMBER   Complete destruction of potato crop.
NOVEMBER   Start of one of the severest winters in living
              memory.

1847

JANUARY   Irish Confederation founded under leadership of
              William Smith O'Brien.
FEBRUARY   Destitute Poor (Ireland) Act provides for the
              setting up of state-aided soup kitchens to
              administer direct relief; famine at its height.
MAY   Death of Daniel O'Connell in Genoa, Italy, *en
              route* to Rome.

1848

FEBRUARY   John Mitchel and followers secede from Irish
            Confederation.
            Revolution in France leads to abdication of King
            Louis-Philippe.

MAY   John Mitchel tried for treason–felony and
            sentenced to fourteen years' transportation in
            Van Diemen's Land (Tasmania). William
            Smith O'Brien acquitted on sedition charges.

JULY   Abortive rising led by Smith O'Brien at
            Ballingarry, County Tipperary.

1849

JULY   Encumbered Estates (Ireland) Act establishes a
            special body to facilitate the sale of mortgaged
            land. Sectarian clashes between Protestants and
            Catholics at Dolly's Brae, near Castlewellan,
            County Down.

1850

FEBRUARY   Archbishop Paul Cullen consecrated Catholic
            Primate of All Ireland.

AUGUST   Irish Tenant League founded in Dublin.

1851

MARCH   Census: population of Ireland, 6,552,385.

AUGUST   Catholic Defence Association formed in
            Dublin.

1852

MARCH   First Saint Patrick's Day parade takes place in
            New York.

1854

NOVEMBER   Catholic University of Ireland opens in
            Dublin.

1858

MARCH James Stephens founds the Irish Revolutionary Brotherhood (IRB), later the Irish Republican Brotherhood, in Dublin.

1859

APRIL John O'Mahony forms the Fenian Brotherhood in New York as the American counterpart to the IRB.

1861

JANUARY Death of Terence Bellew McManus, Young Irelander, in San Francisco.
APRIL American Civil War begins.

1862

JANUARY Harland and Wolff shipbuilding firm established in Belfast.

1864

MARCH Archbishop Paul Cullen issues pastoral letter denouncing Fenianism.

1865

APRIL American Civil War ends.
SEPTEMBER Arrest of leading Fenians in Dublin.
NOVEMBER James Stephens arrested, then escapes from Richmond jail, Dublin.

1866

JUNE Fenian army involved in skirmishes with Canadian forces at Lime Ridgeway.

1867

FEBRUARY Last-minute cancellation of planned Fenian raid on Chester Castle.
MARCH Abortive Fenian rising in parts of Munster and in Dublin area.

JUNE   Clan na Gael, a Fenian organisation, formed in New York.

SEPTEMBER   Police sergeant killed during armed rescue of two Fenian prisoners, Thomas Kelly and Timothy Deasy, from police van in Manchester.

NOVEMBER   William Allen, Michael Larkin and Michael O'Brien (the Manchester Martyrs) hanged in Salford jail for murder of policeman.

DECEMBER   Fenian explosion at Clerkenwell jail, London, causes twelve deaths and numerous injuries.

1869

JULY   Irish Church Act provides for disestablishment and partial disendowment of the Protestant Church of Ireland.

1870

MAY   Irish home rule movement launched by Isaac Butt in Dublin.

AUGUST   Landlord and Tenant (Ireland) Act, Prime Minister William Gladstone's first Land Act.

1871

JANUARY   Church of Ireland becomes a voluntary body under terms of 1869 Act.

1872

JULY   Ballot Act institutes secret voting.

1873

FEBRUARY   Home Rule Confederation of Great Britain founded in Manchester with Isaac Butt as president.

MARCH   Gladstone's Irish University Bill defeated.

NOVEMBER   Home Rule League founded in Dublin.

1874

FEBRUARY   Fifty-nine Irish home rulers returned in general election.

MARCH   Home rule MPs resolve to constitute themselves
           as a separate party at Westminster.
JULY   Isaac Butt's home rule motion defeated in the
           Commons.
           Joseph Biggar and other home rulers begin
           campaign of parliamentary obstruction.

1875
APRIL   Charles Stewart Parnell returned as MP for Meath
           at by-election.

1876
AUGUST   IRB withdraws support from home rule
           movement.

1877
AUGUST   Parnell replaces Isaac Butt as president of Home
           Rule Confederation of Great Britain.
SEPTEMBER Failure of potato harvest in Connacht produces
           fear of famine.
DECEMBER   Michael Davitt released from Dartmoor prison
           on ticket-of-leave.

1878
OCTOBER   Michael Davitt and Clan na Gael leader John
           Devoy call for Fenians, home rulers and agrarian
           agitators to form a New Departure alliance in
           Irish politics.

1879
JANUARY   IRB reject New Departure strategy.
APRIL   Land agitation movement launched at mass
           meeting at Irishtown, County Mayo.
           Start of worst harvest since the Famine in
           Connacht.
AUGUST   National Land League of Mayo founded in
           Castlebar.

OCTOBER   Irish National Land League founded in Dublin
with Parnell as president and Davitt as
secretary.

1880

MAY   Parnell elected chairman of Irish Parliamentary
Party at Westminster.

SEPTEMBER   Parnell calls for ostracism of those who oppose
Land League policies; first used against Mayo
land agent, Captain Charles Boycott.

OCTOBER   Ladies' Land League founded in New York by
Fanny Parnell.

1881

JANUARY   Ladies' Land League launched in Ireland by
Anna Parnell.

FEBRUARY   Davitt arrested and reimprisoned.

AUGUST   Land Law (Ireland) Act, Gladstone's second
Land Act.

SEPTEMBER   Parnell advises Land League to 'test the Act'.

OCTOBER   Parnell arrested and imprisoned in Kilmainham
jail along with other league leaders; Land
League proscribed.

1882

MAY   Parnell and other league leaders released from
jail under the Kilmainham 'Treaty'.
Assassination of Lord Frederick Cavendish
and Thomas Burke in Dublin's
Phoenix Park.

OCTOBER   Foundation of the Irish National League by
Parnell.

1884

NOVEMBER   Gaelic Athletic Association founded at meeting
in Thurles, County Tipperary.

DECEMBER   Reform Act greatly increases Irish electorate.

1885

JANUARY
Fenian dynamite explosions in House of Commons and Tower of London; Parnell makes '*ne plus ultra*' speech in Cork.

MAY
Irish Loyal and Patriotic Union founded to resist home rule movement.

JUNE
Gladstone's government defeated on budget vote; Lord Salisbury forms caretaker minority administration.

AUGUST
Ashbourne Land Purchase Act.

DECEMBER
Parnellites hold balance of power as a result of general election; public disclosure of Gladstone's conversion to home rule.

1886

JANUARY
Formation of Ulster Loyalist Anti-Repeal Union in Belfast.
Salisbury's ministry defeated in Commons vote.

FEBRUARY
Gladstone becomes prime minister for the third time.
Lord Randolph Churchill delivers militant address to Ulster loyalists in Belfast.

APRIL
Gladstone introduces first Home Rule Bill in Commons.

JUNE
Home Rule Bill defeated by thirty votes; parliament dissolved.
Sectarian riots in Belfast.

JULY
Conservatives returned to power under Lord Salisbury.

OCTOBER
Announcement of Plan of Campaign.

1887

MARCH
London *Times* begins series of articles linking Parnellites with agrarian crime.

APRIL
Times publishes alleged letter by Parnell in which he condones 1882 Phoenix Park murders.

1889

FEBRUARY   Special commission set up to investigate allegations against Parnell exposes Richard Pigott as forger of *The Times* letter.

DECEMBER   Captain William O'Shea files for divorce, citing Parnell as co-respondent.

1890

FEBRUARY   Special commission report exonerates Parnell of all serious charges.

NOVEMBER   O'Shea divorce hearing.
Parnell re-elected chairman of Irish Parliamentary Party; Gladstone calls for his resignation; Parnell denounces Gladstone and Liberal alliance.

DECEMBER   Irish Parliamentary Party splits over Parnell's leadership; majority of MPs oppose him.

1891

JUNE   Parnell marries Katharine O'Shea in Sussex.

OCTOBER   Parnell dies in Brighton.

1892

AUGUST   Gladstone appointed prime minister for the fourth time.
National Literary Society founded in Dublin by W.B. Yeats.

1893

FEBRUARY   Gladstone introduces second Home Rule Bill in Commons.

JULY   Gaelic League founded in Dublin by Douglas Hyde and Eoin MacNeill.

SEPTEMBER   Second Home Rule Bill passed by the Commons but rejected by the Lords.

1894

MARCH   Gladstone retires; succeeded as prime minister
by Lord Rosebery.

APRIL   Foundation of Irish Agricultural Organisation
Society.

1896

MAY   Irish Socialist Republican Party founded by
James Connolly.

1898

JANUARY   Start of nationwide celebrations to mark the
centenary of 1798 rising.

AUGUST   Local Government (Ireland) Act creates elected
county and district councils.

1899

MAY   W.B. Yeats's *The Countess Cathleen* becomes the
first production of the Irish Literary Theatre in
Dublin.

OCTOBER   Boer War begins.

1900

APRIL   Queen Victoria visits Ireland.

FEBRUARY   Reunification of the Irish Parliamentary Party
under leadership of John Redmond.

1901

JANUARY   Accession of Edward VII.

1902

DECEMBER   Land Conference of Irish landlords and tenants
opens in Dublin.

1903

AUGUST   Wyndham Land Act.

1904

AUGUST   Formation of pro-devolution Irish Reform
Association.

DECEMBER Abbey Theatre opens in Dublin.

1905

MARCH   Formation of Ulster Unionist Council in Belfast.
First Dungannon Club formed in Belfast by
Bulmer Hobson.

1907

JANUARY Abbey riots following first performance of *The
Playboy of the Western World* by J.M. Synge.

APRIL   Formation of Sinn Féin League.

MAY   James Larkin organises dock strike in Belfast.

JUNE   Liberal government withdraws Irish
Council Bill.

1908

AUGUST   Irish Universities Act.

NOVEMBER Formation of Irish Women's Franchise League.

DECEMBER James Larkin forms Irish Transport and General
Workers' Union.

1909

APRIL   David Lloyd George introduces 'people's
budget'.

NOVEMBER Lords rejects budget.

DECEMBER Birrell's Land Act.

1910

JANUARY   General election gives Irish Parliamentary Party
the balance of power.

FEBRUARY Sir Edward Carson elected leader of Irish
unionists at Westminster.

MAY   Accession of George v.

DECEMBER Irish Parliamentary Party again holds balance of
power after second general election.

1911

AUGUST   Parliament Act curbs powers of House of Lords.
           Formation of Irish Women's Suffrage
           Federation.

NOVEMBER   Andrew Bonar Law becomes Conservative
           leader.

1912

APRIL   Bonar Law pledges his party's support for Ulster
           unionists.
           Prime Minister Herbert Asquith introduces third
           Home Rule Bill in Commons.
           Titanic sinks on its maiden voyage.

SEPTEMBER Ulster unionists sign Solemn League and
           Covenant.

1913

JANUARY   Home Rule Bill passes Commons reading but is
           rejected by the Lords.
           Ulster Volunteer Force (UVF) formed in Belfast.

JULY   Home Rule Bill passes Commons but is again
           rejected by the Lords.

AUGUST   Irish Transport and General Workers' Union
           strike begins in Dublin.

SEPTEMBER Twenty-five thousand Dublin workers locked
           out by employers for refusing to sign
           non-trade-union pledge.

NOVEMBER   Formation of Irish Citizen Army and Irish
           Volunteers in Dublin.

1914

FEBRUARY   Dublin lock-out ends.

MARCH   'Mutiny' among British army officers at the
           Curragh, County Kildare.

APRIL   UVF land German arms at three Ulster ports.

MAY   Home Rule Bill passes Commons for third and
           final time.

JULY Buckingham Palace conference fails to resolve the home rule question.

Irish Volunteers land German arms at Howth, County Dublin.

AUGUST Britain declares war on Germany; First World War begins.

John Redmond pledges Irish support for British war effort.

SEPTEMBER IRB meet to discuss plans for a rising against British rule.

Home Rule Bill receives royal assent but is suspended for duration of the war.

Redmond's appeal to Irish Volunteers to join the British army in speech at Woodenbridge, County Wicklow, leads to split in the Volunteers.

1915

MAY Edward Carson joins Herbert Asquith's coalition government as attorney general.

DECEMBER IRB sets up secret military council to plan rising.

1916

APRIL Rising takes place in Dublin during Easter week.

MAY Fifteen rebel leaders executed in Kilmainham jail.

JULY 36th (Ulster) Division sustains heavy casualties at Battle of the Somme.

AUGUST Roger Casement executed at Pentonville prison.

DECEMBER David Lloyd George becomes prime minister of coalition government.

1917

FEBRUARY Count Plunkett wins North Roscommon by-election for Sinn Féin.

JULY Eamon de Valera wins East Clare by-election for Sinn Féin.

First meeting of Irish Convention in Dublin.

OCTOBER   De Valera elected president of Sinn Féin and of
the Irish Volunteers.

1918

FEBRUARY   Representation of the People Act enfranchises
almost all men over twenty-one years of age
and most women over thirty.

APRIL   Military Service Bill threatens conscription for
Ireland and provokes widespread national
condemnation.

NOVEMBER   Armistice between Germany and Allied powers
ends First World War.

DECEMBER   Sinn Féin wins 73 of Ireland's 105 seats in general
election.

1919

JANUARY   First meeting of Dáil Éireann in Mansion House
in Dublin.
Irish Volunteer unit kills two policemen at
Soloheadbeg, County Tipperary; Anglo-Irish
War begins.

APRIL   De Valera elected president of Dáil.

AUGUST   Irish Volunteers become known as Irish
Republican Army (IRA).

SEPTEMBER   Dáil declared illegal.

1920

FEBRUARY   Government of Ireland Act introduced in
Commons.

MARCH   First of the Black and Tans arrive in Ireland.

SEPTEMBER   Black and Tans raid Balbriggan, County
Dublin.

NOVEMBER   Bloody Sunday in Dublin.

DECEMBER   Black and Tans and Auxiliaries sack Cork city
centre.
Government of Ireland Act partitions
Ireland.

1921

FEBRUARY James Craig succeeds Lord Carson as leader
of the Ulster unionists.

MAY Custom House in Dublin burned by IRA.

JUNE George V opens Northern Ireland parliament at
Belfast City Hall.

JULY Truce between IRA and British army.

AUGUST Second Dáil assembles in Dublin.

OCTOBER Anglo–Irish conference begins in London.

DECEMBER Anglo–Irish Treaty signed in London;
Dáil debate on treaty begins.

1922

JANUARY Dáil approves treaty by 64 votes to 57, de Valera
resigns presidency, which is taken over by Arthur
Griffith; provisional government takes control
under chairmanship of Michael Collins.

MARCH IRA splits over the treaty.
Craig–Collins pact agreed in London.

APRIL Anti-treaty forces under Rory O'Connor seize
Four Courts in Dublin.

MAY Collins–de Valera pact agreed.

JUNE Pro-treaty Sinn Féin wins large majority in
southern general election.
Bombardment of anti-treaty IRA garrison in the
Four Courts by provisional government troops
triggers Irish Civil War.

JULY Death toll from sectarian violence in Northern
Ireland since July 1920 exceeds 550.

AUGUST Arthur Griffith dies of cerebral haemorrhage.
Michael Collins killed in ambush at Béal na
mBláth, County Cork.

SEPTEMBER Third Dáil assembles in Dublin; William T.
Cosgrave elected president.
Abolition of proportional representation in
Northern Ireland local elections.

NOVEMBER Execution of anti-treaty IRA prisoners in
Kilmainham jail begins.

DECEMBER Irish Free State comes into existence; Northern Ireland parliament exercises its right to opt out of the Free State under terms of the treaty.

1923

MARCH Formation of pro-treaty Cumann na nGaedheal by William T. Cosgrave.

APRIL Liam Lynch, leader of anti-treaty IRA, killed by Free State troops in County Waterford.

MAY De Valera's appeal to anti-treatyite forces to cease fighting ends Civil War.

AUGUST Cumann na nGaedheal wins majority of seats in first Free State general election.

SEPTEMBER Fourth Dáil assembles; Cosgrave elected president of the executive council.
Irish Free State admitted to League of Nations.

NOVEMBER W.B. Yeats awarded Nobel prize for literature.

1924

MARCH 'Mutiny' by disaffected IRA veterans within the Irish Free State army.

NOVEMBER First meeting of the Boundary Commission in London.

1925

NOVEMBER Boundary Commission findings leaked by *Morning Post* newspaper; Eoin MacNeill resigns from commission.

DECEMBER William T. Cosgrave, Stanley Baldwin and James Craig sign agreement to suppress Boundary Commission report and retain existing border.

1926

MAY Fianna Fáil party launched by de Valera in Dublin.

1927

JULY   Kevin O'Higgins, minister for justice,
            assassinated by republicans in Dublin.
AUGUST   Fianna Fáil deputies, led by de Valera, sign the
            parliamentary oath and take their seats in
            the Dáil.

1929

APRIL   Abolition of proportional representation in all
            Northern Ireland elections.
JULY   Censorship of Publications Act passed by the
            Dáil.

1931

DECEMBER   Statute of Westminster passed by UK parliament.

1932

MARCH   De Valera forms first Fianna Fáil government.
JUNE   Irish government's decision to withhold
            payment of land annuities to Britain triggers
            economic war between the two countries.
NOVEMBER   Prince of Wales opens Stormont, the new home
            of the Northern Ireland parliament.

1933

MAY   Dáil passes Act removing oath of allegiance from
            the Irish constitution.
            Special Powers Act passed by Stormont
            government.
SEPTEMBER   Formation of United Ireland party, later known
            as Fine Gael, from Cumann na nGaedheal and
            other parties.

1935

FEBRUARY   Free State government bans importation and sale
            of contraceptives.

1936

JANUARY   Accession of Edward VIII.

MAY   Inaugural flight of Aer Lingus, national Irish airline.

JUNE   Free State government declares IRA illegal.

DECEMBER   Abdication of Edward VIII; succeeded by George VI.

            Dáil passes legislation removing all references to the crown from the Irish constitution and limiting the crown's role in Irish diplomatic affairs.

1937

JUNE   De Valera's new constitution approved by the Dáil.

JULY   Constitution ratified by referendum.

DECEMBER   Constitution comes into effect.

            Irish Free State becomes Éire.

1938

APRIL   De Valera and Neville Chamberlain sign Anglo-Irish Agreement in London, ending the economic war.

JUNE   Douglas Hyde inaugurated as first president of Éire.

1939

JANUARY   IRA begins bombing campaign in England.

SEPTEMBER   Germany invades Poland; de Valera announces his government's intention to remain neutral during the war; Britain and France declare war on Germany; start of 'the Emergency' in Éire.

1940

JANUARY   Irish government introduces emergency. legislation to combat IRA threat.

NOVEMBER   J.M. Andrews succeeds Lord Craigavon as prime
             minister of Northern Ireland.

1941

APRIL   Over seven hundred people killed in first
             German air raids on Northern Ireland.
MAY   Over thirty people killed by German bomb in
             the North Strand area of Dublin.

1942

JANUARY   First American troops arrive in Northern
             Ireland.

1943

MAY   Basil Brooke succeeds J.M. Andrews as prime
             minister of Northern Ireland.

1945

MAY   De Valera expresses formal condolences to
             German envoy in Ireland on news of Hitler's
             death.
             End of the war in Europe.
JUNE   Sean T. O'Kelly elected president of Éire.
AUGUST   Japan's surrender ends the Second World War.

1946

JULY   Formation of Clann na Poblachta by Seán
             MacBride.
AUGUST   Éire's application to join United Nations
             Organisation (UN) vetoed by USSR.

1948

FEBRUARY   Fianna Fáil replaced by coalition government
             under Fine Gael leader John A. Costello.
SEPTEMBER   During a visit to Canada, Costello announces
             government's intention to repeal 1936 External
             Relations Act and declare Éire a republic.
DECEMBER   Republic of Ireland Act passed by the Dáil.

1949

APRIL   Éire becomes Republic of Ireland and leaves the Commonwealth.

JUNE   Ireland Act passed at Westminster, guaranteeing Northern Ireland's position within the United Kingdom.

1951

APRIL   Health minister Dr Noel Browne resigns following episcopal condemnation of his 'mother-and-child' scheme.

JUNE   Fianna Fáil returns to power under de Valera.

1952

FEBRUARY   Accession of Elizabeth II.

1954

APRIL   Flags and Emblems Act prohibits public interference with Union Jack in Northern Ireland and bans display of the tricolour.

JUNE   Costello forms second coalition government.

1955

DECEMBER   Republic admitted to the United Nations Organisation.

1956

NOVEMBER   Start of Operation Harvest, IRA campaign against the Northern Ireland state.

1957

JANUARY   Two IRA members killed in border raid in County Fermanagh.

MARCH   Fianna Fáil government takes office under de Valera.
    European Economic Community institutes under Treaty of Rome.

1958

JUNE   First Irish troops depart for UN duty in Lebanon.

JULY   Industrial Development Act seeks to encourage
            foreign capital investment in Republic.

NOVEMBER   First Programme for Economic Expansion
            published in Dublin.

1959

JUNE   De Valera elected president of Ireland.
            Sean Lemass becomes taoiseach.
            Republic electorate rejects proposal to abolish
            proportional representation.

1960

NOVEMBER   Ten Irish soldiers killed while on UN duty in the
            Congo.

1961

AUGUST   Republic makes unsuccessful application for
            EEC membership.

DECEMBER   First broadcast of Irish television service, Radio
            Telefís Éireann.

1962

FEBRUARY   IRA calls off Operation Harvest.

1963

MARCH   Terence O'Neill succeeds Lord Brookeborough
            as Northern Ireland prime minister.

JUNE   Official visit to the Republic by US President
            John F. Kennedy.

1964

JANUARY   Campaign for Social Justice launched in
            Northern Ireland.

SEPTEMBER   Riots in Belfast during general election
            campaign.

1965

JANUARY   Sean Lemass and Terence O'Neill meet in
          Belfast.

FEBRUARY Nationalist Party assumes role of official
          opposition at Stormont.
          Lemass and O'Neill meet in Dublin.

DECEMBER Anglo-Irish Free Trade Area Agreement signed.

1966

MARCH   Nelson's Pillar in Dublin destroyed by
          explosion.

APRIL   Fiftieth anniversary of Easter Rising
          commemorated in both parts of Ireland.

JUNE   Three Catholics shot, one of them dead,
          in Belfast by the Ulster Volunteer Force.

NOVEMBER Jack Lynch succeeds Lemass as taoiseach.

1967

JANUARY   Formation of Northern Ireland Civil Rights
          Association (NICRA).

MAY   Republic again unsuccessfully applies for
          EEC membership.

1968

AUGUST   NICRA march from Coalisland to Dungannon to
          protest against anti-Catholic discrimination.

OCTOBER   Civil rights marchers clash with police in Derry,
          followed by rioting.
          People's Democracy, a left-wing student group,
          formed in Belfast.

1969

JANUARY   People's Democracy march from Belfast to
          Derry attacked by loyalists at Burntollet Bridge
          near Derry.

APRIL   Riots in Derry and Belfast.
          O'Neill resigns as prime minister; succeeded by
          James Chichester-Clark.

AUGUST   Riots in the Bogside area of Derry and in Belfast.
Taoiseach Lynch threatens intervention to
protect Catholic minority.
First British troops arrive in Derry and Belfast.

1970

JANUARY   IRA splits into Official and Provisional factions.
APRIL   Disbandment of B Specials.
MAY   Taoiseach Lynch dismisses Charles Haughey and
Neil Blaney from the cabinet over allegations of
arms smuggling.
JUNE   Provisional IRA engages in first sustained military
action.
Conservative government comes to power
under Edward Heath.
JULY   Army imposes curfew on Catholic Falls Road
area of Belfast.
AUGUST   Formation of Social Democratic and Labour
Party (SDLP) in Belfast.
OCTOBER   Haughey acquitted on charges of conspiring to
import arms.

1971

FEBRUARY   Provisional IRA kills first British soldier of the
Troubles.
MARCH   James Chichester-Clark resigns as Northern
Ireland prime minister; succeeded by Brian
Faulkner.
JULY   SDLP withdraws from Stormont in protest at
failure to inquire into the deaths of two civilians
killed by the army in Derry.
AUGUST   Internment without trial introduced in Northern
Ireland.
SEPTEMBER   Formation of Ulster Defence Association (UDA).
OCTOBER   Formation of the Democratic Unionist Party.

1972

JANUARY   Bloody Sunday in Derry, thirteen people killed
by British paratroopers.

FEBRUARY	British embassy burned down by protesting crowd in Dublin. Tribunal of inquiry into Bloody Sunday set up under Lord Widgery.
MARCH	British government suspends Stormont parliament and imposes direct rule from Westminster; William Whitelaw appointed secretary of state for Northern Ireland.
APRIL	Widgery Report exonerates the army for Bloody Sunday killings and blames NICRA for organising an illegal march.
JUNE	Introduction of special category status for republican and loyalist prisoners in Northern Ireland, acknowledging the political nature of their crimes.
JULY	Bloody Friday in Belfast, eleven killed by IRA bombs.
DECEMBER	Referendum in the Republic supports the removal of the special position of the Catholic Church from the constitution.

1973

JANUARY	Republic and Britain become members of the EEC.
MARCH	Fine Gael–Labour coalition government takes office under Fine Gael leader Liam Cosgrave.
MAY	Erskine Childers elected president of Ireland.
JUNE	Ulster Freedom Fighters (UFF), a cover name for the UDA, kill Senator Paddy Wilson in Belfast.
JULY	First meeting of Northern Ireland assembly ends in disorder.
DECEMBER	British and Irish premiers sign the Sunningdale Agreement. Republic's ban on importation of contraceptives declared unconstitutional.

1974

JANUARY   Northern Ireland power-sharing Executive takes
            office.

MARCH   Labour government comes to power in Britain
            under Harold Wilson.

MAY   Ulster Workers' Council strike forces resignation
            of power-sharing Executive and collapse of
            Sunningdale Agreement.
            Thirty-three people killed by loyalist car bombs
            in Dublin and Monaghan.

OCTOBER   Five people killed in IRA pub bombing in
            Guildford.

NOVEMBER   Twenty-one people killed in IRA pub bombings
            in Birmingham.
            British government introduces Prevention of
            Terrorism Act.

DECEMBER   Cearbhall Ó Dálaigh elected president of Ireland.
            Irish National Liberation Army (INLA) set up as
            military wing of Irish Republican Socialist Party
            (IRSP).
            Prevention of Terrorism Act applied to
            Northern Ireland.

1975

FEBRUARY   IRA declares an indefinite cease-fire; liaison takes
            place between Sinn Féin and British government
            representatives.

APRIL   First breach of IRA cease-fire.

SEPTEMBER   IRA cease-fire ends.

DECEMBER   Internment without trial in Northern Ireland
            ends.

1976

MARCH   Abolition of special category political status in
            Northern Ireland prisons.

APRIL   Harold Wilson resigns as prime minister;
            succeeded by James Callaghan.

JULY   British ambassador Christopher Ewart–Biggs killed by IRA landmine in County Dublin.

AUGUST   Launch of the Peace People movement in Belfast.

SEPTEMBER   First republican prisoner to be refused special category status goes on 'blanket' protest in the H-blocks at the Maze prison.

OCTOBER   President Ó Dálaigh resigns following public criticism from Republic's defence minister; succeeded by Patrick Hillery.

1977

MAY   United Unionist Action Council strike fails to stop industry and commerce in Northern Ireland.

JULY   Fianna Fáil government takes office under Jack Lynch.

AUGUST   Queen Elizabeth makes Jubilee visit to Northern Ireland.

OCTOBER   Mairead Corrigan and Betty Williams, founders of the Peace People, awarded Nobel peace prize.

1978

JANUARY   European Court of Human Rights rules that IRA internees were subjected to 'inhuman and degrading treatment' in Northern Ireland in 1971.

FEBRUARY   Twelve people die as a result of IRA bomb at the La Mon House Hotel, County Down.

1979

MARCH   Republic joins the European Monetary System and breaks with sterling.
Airey Neave, Conservative spokesman on Northern Ireland, killed by INLA car bomb in Westminster.

MAY   Conservative Party returns to power under Margaret Thatcher.

AUGUST   Earl Mountbatten killed by IRA bomb at
              Mullaghmore, County Sligo.
              Eighteen British soldiers killed by IRA bomb at
              Warrenpoint, County Down.
SEPTEMBER   Pope John Paul II visits the Republic.
DECEMBER   Jack Lynch resigns as taoiseach; succeeded by
              Charles Haughey.

1980

OCTOBER   Seven republican prisoners in the Maze begin a
              hunger strike, demanding the right to wear their
              own clothes.
DECEMBER   Thatcher and Haughey meet for Anglo-Irish
              summit in Dublin at which they agree to discuss
              'the totality of relationships within these islands'.
              Maze hunger strike ends.

1981

MARCH   Republican prisoners in the Maze, led by Bobby
              Sands, begin new hunger strike aimed at
              regaining special category political status.
APRIL   Sands wins Fermanagh–South Tyrone
              by-election.
MAY   Death of Sands after sixty-six days on hunger
              strike provokes riots and demonstrations in both
              parts of Ireland.
JUNE   Formation of Fine Gael–Labour coalition in the
              Republic under Fine Gael leader Garret
              FitzGerald.
SEPTEMBER   Taoiseach FitzGerald launches his 'constitutional
              crusade' in the Republic.
OCTOBER   Maze hunger strike ends, a total of ten republican
              prisoners having died since May; government
              subsequently concedes prisoners' demand to
              wear their own clothes.
NOVEMBER   Ulster Unionist MP Robert Bradford killed by
              the IRA.

1982

FEBRUARY   Fianna Fáil minority government takes office
under Charles Haughey.

MAY   Rift develops between Irish and British
governments following the sinking of the
Argentinian battleship *General Belgrano* during
the Falklands War.

JULY   Eight British soldiers killed by IRA bombs in
London.

NOVEMBER   Fine Gael–Labour coalition returns to power
under Garret FitzGerald.
First meeting of new Northern Ireland assembly
takes place in Belfast.

DECEMBER   Seventeen people, including eleven British
soldiers, killed by INLA bomb at Droppin'
Well bar in Ballykelly, County Londonderry.

1983

MAY   First meeting of New Ireland Forum takes place
at Dublin Castle.

JUNE   Gerry Adams elected Sinn Féin MP for West
Belfast.

SEPTEMBER   Referendum in the Republic supports
anti-abortion constitutional amendment.
Mass escape of thirty-eight republican prisoners
from the Maze.

1984

MAY   Publication of New Ireland Forum report.

JUNE   Official visit to the Republic by US President
Ronald Reagan.

OCTOBER   Five people killed by IRA bomb at the Grand
Hotel, Brighton, during Conservative Party
conference.

NOVEMBER   Prime Minister Thatcher rejects all three options
of Forum report following Anglo-Irish summit
meeting with Taoiseach FitzGerald at Chequers.

1985

FEBRUARY   Nine RUC officers killed in IRA mortar attack on Newry police station.

NOVEMBER   British and Irish premiers sign the Anglo-Irish Agreement at Hillsborough Castle, County Down; widespread loyalist protests against the agreement throughout Northern Ireland.

DECEMBER   All fifteen unionist MPs resign their seats in protest at the agreement.
Progressive Democrat party founded in Dublin.

1986

JANUARY   Fourteen of the fifteen unionist MPs regain their seats in by-elections.

JUNE   Referendum in the Republic rejects the introduction of civil divorce.
Northern Ireland assembly dissolved.

NOVEMBER   Sinn Féin votes to end abstentionist policy from the Dáil; dissenting minority leave to form Republican Sinn Féin.

1987

FEBRUARY   Fianna Fáil minority government takes office under Charles Haughey.

MAY   Eight IRA men shot dead during raid on Loughgall RUC station in County Armagh.
Single European Act ratified by referendum in the Republic.

NOVEMBER   Eleven people killed by IRA bomb in Enniskillen, County Fermanagh, during Remembrance Day ceremony.

1988

JANUARY   Start of talks process between John Hume and Gerry Adams.

MARCH   Three IRA members shot dead in Gibraltar by
            SAS unit; five people killed, including two
            British soldiers, during two subsequent funerals
            in Belfast.

AUGUST   Eight British soldiers killed by IRA landmine near
            Ballygawley, County Tyrone.

OCTOBER   British government imposes broadcasting ban on
            paramilitary groups.

NOVEMBER   Rift develops between Irish and British
            governments over extradition to Britain of
            Father Patrick Ryan.

1989

JULY   Fianna Fáil–Progressive Democrat coalition
            government takes office under Charles Haughey.

SEPTEMBER   Ten British soldiers killed by IRA bomb at army
            base in Kent.

OCTOBER   Release on appeal of the Guildford Four after
            fourteen years in prison.

1990

APRIL   Relations between Irish and British governments
            deteriorate following row over the extradition to
            Northern Ireland of former MP Owen Carron.

NOVEMBER   Mary Robinson elected president of Ireland.
            John Major succeeds Margaret Thatcher as
            British prime minister.

1991

FEBRUARY   IRA mortar bomb attack on 10 Downing Street.

MARCH   Release on appeal of the Birmingham Six after
            sixteen years in prison.
            Secretary of State Peter Brooke announces his
            formula for inter-party talks in Northern Ireland.

JULY   Brooke suspends the inter-party talks process
            after less than three weeks of negotiations.

DECEMBER   IRA launches Christmas bombing campaign in
            Britain.

1992

JANUARY   Eight Protestant workers killed by IRA bomb
            near Cookstown, County Tyrone.

FEBRUARY   Five Catholics shot dead by UFF gunmen on the
            Ormeau Road, Belfast.
            Albert Reynolds succeeds Charles Haughey as
            taoiseach.
            'X' case abortion controversy in the Republic.

MARCH   Formation of Democratic Left following split in
            the Workers' Party.

APRIL   Conservative Party returns to power under John
            Major.
            Inter-party talks reconvene in Northern Ireland
            under the auspices of Sir Patrick Mayhew, the
            new secretary of state.

MAY   Eamonn Casey resigns as Bishop of Galway.

JUNE   Maastricht treaty ratified by referendum in the
            Republic.

AUGUST   British government proscribes the UDA.
            Death of 3,000th victim of the Troubles.

NOVEMBER   Collapse of the Northern Ireland talks process
            after unionists withdraw.
            Referendum in the Republic supports the right
            of women to travel abroad for abortion but
            rejects proposal to allow restricted form of
            abortion in Ireland.

1993

JANUARY   Fianna Fáil–Labour coalition government takes
            office under Albert Reynolds.

MARCH   Two young boys killed by IRA bomb in
            Warrington, Cheshire; an estimated twenty
            thousand people attend peace rally in Dublin.

APRIL   IRA bomb extensively damages NatWest tower
            in London.

MAY   President Robinson meets Queen Elizabeth at
            Buckingham Palace, the first ever meeting
            between an Irish president and a British
            monarch.

JUNE   President Robinson makes a visit to Belfast, during which she shakes hands with Gerry Adams.

Republic decriminalises homosexual acts between consenting adults over the age of seventeen.

OCTOBER   Irish government receives details of the Hume–Adams peace initiative.

Ten people killed by IRA bomb on the Shankill Road, Belfast; seven die in retaliatory UFF attack in Greysteel, County Londonderry.

NOVEMBER   Details emerge of secret three-year contacts between British government and Sinn Féin representatives.

DECEMBER   Premiers Major and Reynolds issue Downing Street Declaration in London.

1994

JANUARY   Sinn Féin seeks clarification of Downing Street Declaration.

Broadcasting ban on Sinn Féin lifted in the Republic.

FEBRUARY   Gerry Adams visits US on a visa authorised by President Clinton.

MARCH   IRA launches mortar attack on Heathrow Airport.

AUGUST   Declaration of IRA cease-fire.

SEPTEMBER   British government seeks confirmation that cease-fire is 'permanent'.

Taoiseach Reynolds meets Hume and Adams in Dublin.

OCTOBER   Combined Loyalist Military Command declares cease-fire.

British government insists on decommissioning of IRA arms as a precondition for Sinn Féin's entry into all-party talks.

Forum for Peace and Reconciliation opens in Dublin.

NOVEMBER	Fianna Fáil–Labour coalition collapses over extradition row involving new High Court president.
DECEMBER	Formation of 'rainbow' coalition government under Fine Gael leader John Bruton.

1995

FEBRUARY	Publication of the Frameworks Documents.
MARCH	Adams attends Saint Patrick's Day reception at the White House, Washington.
MAY	First official meeting between Sinn Féin representatives and a British government minister takes place at Stormont.
JULY	Stand-off between Orange marchers and the RUC at Drumcree, County Armagh, leads to the so-called 'siege of Drumcree'.
SEPTEMBER	David Trimble elected leader of the Ulster Unionist Party.
OCTOBER	Seamus Heaney awarded the Nobel prize for literature.
NOVEMBER	Referendum in the Republic supports the legalisation of civil divorce.
	Premiers Major and Bruton launch their twin-track strategy on the eve of President Clinton's three-day official visit to both parts of Ireland.
DECEMBER	International body on arms decommissioning set up under chairmanship of former US Senator George Mitchell.

1996

JANUARY	Publication of the Mitchell report.
FEBRUARY	IRA cease-fire ends with a bomb explosion at Canary Wharf in London.
MAY	Elections to the Northern Ireland forum.
JUNE	President Robinson makes official visit to Britain.
	Sinn Féin excluded from start of all-party talks chaired by Senator Mitchell.

IRA bomb in Manchester causes widespread injuries and damage.

JULY   Stand-off between Orange marchers and the RUC at Drumcree for second consecutive year; march eventually proceeds following reversal of original decision to re-route.

1997

FEBRUARY   Civil divorce becomes legal in the Republic.
McCracken tribunal set up to investigate 'payments to politicians' scandal in the Republic.

MAY   Labour Party returns to power under Tony Blair.
Prime Minister Blair 'apologises' for Britain's role in the Famine.

JUNE   Fianna Fáil–Progressive Democrat coalition government takes office under Bertie Ahern.

JULY   Decision to allow Drumcree Orange parade to proceed through Garvaghy Road provokes widespread nationalist anger and rioting in Northern Ireland.
Renewal of IRA cease-fire.

SEPTEMBER   Sinn Féin agree to Mitchell principles and is admitted to all-party talks at Stormont.

OCTOBER   Prime Minister Blair meets Adams during visit to Belfast.
Mary McAleese elected president of Ireland.

DECEMBER   Prime Minister Blair meets Sinn Féin delegation at 10 Downing Street.
Loyalist Volunteer Force leader Billy Wright assassinated by republican inmates in the Maze.

1998

JANUARY   Secretary of State Mo Mowlam meets loyalist inmates in the Maze.

FEBRUARY   Sinn Féin excluded from the talks process for a two-week period.

APRIL   Good Friday Agreement signed at Castle Buildings, Stormont.

MAY   Referendums in both parts of Ireland ratify the
Good Friday Agreement.

JUNE   Elections to the Northern Ireland assembly.

JULY   David Trimble elected First Minister designate
of Northern Ireland at inaugural meeting of the
assembly.
Lengthy stand-off between Orangemen and
security forces at Drumcree.
Three children killed in loyalist petrol-bomb
attack in Ballymoney, County Antrim.

AUGUST   Twenty-nine people killed as a result of
Real IRA car bomb in Omagh, County Tyrone;
British and Irish governments introduce
emergency anti-terrorist legislation.

SEPTEMBER   Sinn Féin statement says violence is 'over, done
with and gone'.
Official visit by President Clinton to both parts
of Ireland.
First face-to-face meeting between Trimble and
Adams.

OCTOBER   John Hume and David Trimble awarded Nobel
peace prize.

NOVEMBER   President McAleese and Queen Elizabeth unveil
memorial in Flanders to Irish soldiers killed
in First World War.
Tony Blair becomes first British prime minister
to address both houses of the Irish parliament.

DECEMBER   Loyalist Volunteer Force becomes first
paramilitary group to decommission some arms.
Northern Ireland political parties and the two
governments agree on numbers of departments
in new Northern Ireland administration and on
areas of cross-border co-operation.

APPENDIX

BRITISH HEADS OF GOVERNMENT

Until the eighteenth century, public offices in Britain were so devolved that it is often very difficult, even arbitrary, to decide who should be regarded as head of government. The epithet 'prime minister' was first applied pejoratively to Robert Walpole who, as first lord of the Treasury, was the leading member of the government between 1721 and 1742. Henry Pelham achieved similar status as first lord from 1743 to 1754. The office of prime minister was firmly established by the time of William Pitt the Younger, though the title was not formally recognised until 1905.

Party labels were often arbitrary in the late-eighteenth and early-nineteenth centuries. Even in the period 1830–68, the designations Whig, Tory, Liberal and Conservative were not always used consistently. Titles indicated here are those held when the prime ministers left office.

1770	February	Lord North
1782	March	Charles Wentworth, 2nd Marquis of Rockingham
1782	July	William Petty, 3rd Earl of Shelburne
1783	April	William Cavendish Bentinck, 3rd Duke of Portland
1783	December	William Pitt the Younger
1801	March	Henry Addington
1804	May	William Pitt the Younger
1806	February	William Grenville, 1st Baron Grenville
1807	March	William Cavendish Bentinck, 3rd Duke of Portland
1809	October	Spencer Perceval
1812	June	Robert Jenkinson, 2nd Earl of Liverpool
1827	April	George Canning

1827	August	Frederick Robinson, Viscount Goderich
1828	January	Arthur Wellesley, 1st Duke of Wellington (Tory)
1830	November	Charles Grey, 2nd Earl Grey (Whig)
1834	July	William Lamb, 2nd Viscount Melbourne (Whig)
1834	December	Sir Robert Peel (Conservative)
1835	April	William Lamb, 2nd Viscount Melbourne (Whig)
1841	August	Sir Robert Peel (Conservative)
1846	July	Lord John Russell (Whig)
1852	February	Edward Stanley, 14th Earl of Derby (Conservative)
1852	December	George Gordon, 4th Earl of Aberdeen
1855	February	Henry Temple, 3rd Viscount Palmerston
1858	February	Edward Stanley, 14th Earl of Derby (Conservative)
1859	June	Henry Temple, 3rd Viscount Palmerston
1865	October	1st Earl (formerly Lord John) Russell (Whig)
1866	June	Edward Stanley, 14th Earl of Derby (Conservative)
1868	February	Benjamin Disraeli (Conservative)
1868	December	William Gladstone (Liberal)
1874	February	Benjamin Disraeli, 1st Earl of Beaconsfield (Conservative)
1880	April	William Gladstone (Liberal)
1885	June	Robert Cecil, 3rd Marquis of Salisbury (Conservative)
1886	February	William Gladstone (Liberal)
1886	July	Robert Cecil, 3rd Marquis of Salisbury (Conservative)
1892	August	William Gladstone (Liberal)
1894	March	Archibald Primrose, 5th Earl of Rosebery (Liberal)
1895	June	Robert Cecil, 3rd Marquis of Salisbury (Conservative-Unionist)
1902	July	Arthur Balfour (Conservative-Unionist)
1905	December	Sir Henry Campbell-Bannerman (Liberal)
1908	April	Herbert Asquith (Liberal)

1915	May	Herbert Asquith (Coalition)
1916	December	David Lloyd George (Coalition)
1922	October	Andrew Bonar Law (Conservative)
1923	April	Stanley Baldwin (Conservative)
1924	January	Ramsay MacDonald (Labour)
1924	November	Stanley Baldwin (Conservative)
1929	June	Ramsay MacDonald (Labour)
1931	August	Ramsay MacDonald (National)
1935	June	Stanley Baldwin (National)
1937	May	Neville Chamberlain (National)
1940	May	Winston Churchill (Coalition)
1945	July	Clement Attlee (Labour)
1951	October	Sir Winston Churchill (Conservative)
1955	April	Sir Anthony Eden (Conservative)
1957	January	Harold Macmillan (Conservative)
1963	October	Sir Alec Douglas-Home (Conservative)
1964	October	Harold Wilson (Labour)
1970	June	Edward Heath (Conservative)
1974	March	Harold Wilson (Labour)
1976	April	James Callaghan (Labour)
1979	May	Margaret Thatcher (Conservative)
1990	November	John Major (Conservative)
1997	May	Tony Blair (Labour)

IRISH HEADS OF GOVERNMENT

Irish Free State (Éire after December 1937)

1922	December	William T. Cosgrave (Pro-treaty Sinn Féin)
1923	August	William T. Cosgrave (Cumann na nGaedheal)
1932	March	Eamon de Valera (Fianna Fáil)
1948	February	John A. Costello (Fine Gael-led coalition)

Republic of Ireland (after April 1949)

1951	June	Eamon de Valera (Fianna Fáil)
1954	June	John A. Costello (Fine Gael-led coalition)
1957	March	Eamon de Valera (Fianna Fáil)
1959	June	Sean Lemass (Fianna Fáil)
1966	November	Jack Lynch (Fianna Fáil)
1973	March	Liam Cosgrave (Fine Gael–Labour coalition)
1977	June	Jack Lynch (Fianna Fáil)
1979	December	Charles Haughey (Fianna Fáil)
1981	June	Garret FitzGerald (Fine Gael–Labour coalition)
1982	March	Charles Haughey (Fianna Fáil)
1982	November	Garret FitzGerald (Fine Gael–Labour coalition)
1987	February	Charles Haughey (Fianna Fáil)
1989	July	Charles Haughey (Fianna Fáil–Progressive Democrat coalition)
1992	February	Albert Reynolds (Fianna Fáil–Labour coalition)
1994	December	John Bruton (Fine Gael-led 'rainbow' coalition)
1997	June	Bertie Ahern (Fianna Fáil–Progressive Democrat coalition)

NORTHERN IRISH HEADS OF GOVERNMENT

1921	June	James Craig, 1st Viscount Craigavon (Unionist)
1940	November	J.M. Andrews (Unionist)
1943	May	Basil Brooke, 1st Viscount Brookeborough (Unionist)
1963	March	Terence O'Neill (Unionist)
1969	May	James Chichester-Clark (Unionist)
1971	March	Brian Faulkner (Unionist)
1972	March	Parliament suspended, direct rule introduced

FURTHER READING

Ardagh, J. *Ireland and the Irish: Portrait of a Changing Society* (London, 1994)

Arthur, P. and K. Jeffrey. *Northern Ireland Since 1968* (Oxford, 1988)

Bardon, J. *A History of Ulster* (Belfast, 1992)

Bartlett, T. *The Rise and Fall of the Irish Nation: The Catholic Question, 1690–1830* (Dublin, 1992)

Beresford, D. *Ten Men Dead: The Story of the 1981 Irish Hunger Strike* (London, 1982)

Bowyer Bell, J. *The Irish Troubles: A Generation of Violence, 1967–1992* (Dublin, 1993)

Boyce, D.G. *Nineteenth-Century Ireland: The Search for Stability* (Dublin, 1990)

Boyce, D.G. and A. O'Day. *Irish Nationalism: 1798 to the Present* (London, 1999)

Brown, T. *Ireland: A Social and Cultural History, 1922–1985* (London, 1985)

Connolly, S. *Religion, Law and Power: The Making of Protestant Ireland, 1660–1760* (Oxford, 1992)

Coogan, T.P. *The Troubles: Ireland's Ordeal 1966–1996 and the Search for Peace* (London, 1995)

Curtis, I. *The Cause of Ireland: From the United Irishmen to Partition* (Belfast, 1994)

Dickson, D., D. Keogh and K. Whelan (eds.). *The United Irishmen: Republicanism, Radicalism and Rebellion* (Dublin, 1993)

Douglas, R., L. Harte and J. O'Hara. *Drawing Conclusions: A Cartoon History of Anglo-Irish Relations, 1798–1998* (Belfast, 1998)

Elliott, M. *Partners in Revolution: The United Irishmen and France* (London, 1992)

Fitzpatrick, D. *The Two Irelands, 1912–1939* (Oxford, 1998)

Foster, R.F. *Modern Ireland: 1600–1972* (London, 1988)

Garvin, T. *Nationalist Revolutionaries in Ireland, 1858–1928* (Oxford, 1987)

Gibbons, L. *Transformations in Irish Culture* (Cork, 1996)

Harkness, D. *Ireland in the Twentieth Century: Divided Island* (London, 1996)

Hopkinson, M. *Green Against Green: The Irish Civil War* (Dublin, 1988)

Hoppen, K.T. *Ireland Since 1800: Conflict and Conformity* (London, 1998)

Hussey, G. *Ireland Today: Anatomy of a Changing State* (London, 1995)

Kelly, J. *Prelude to Union: Anglo-Irish Politics in the 1780s* (Cork, 1992)

Kenny, M. *Goodbye to Catholic Ireland* (London, 1997)

Keogh, D. *Twentieth-Century Ireland: Nation and State* (Dublin, 1994)

Keogh, D. and N. Furlong. *The Mighty Wave: The 1798 Rebellion in Wexford* (Dublin, 1996)

Kiberd, D. *Inventing Ireland: The Literature of the Modern Nation* (London, 1995)

Kinealy, C. *This Great Calamity: The Irish Famine 1845–52* (Dublin, 1994)

Laffan, M. *The Partition of Ireland: 1911–1925* (Dundalk, 1983)

Lee, J.J. *The Modernisation of Irish Society: 1848–1918* (Dublin, 1992)
  Ireland 1912–1985: Politics and Society (Cambridge, 1989)

Luddy, M. *Women in Ireland, 1800–1918: A Documentary History* (Cork, 1995)

Lydon, J. *The Making of Ireland: From Ancient Times to the Present* (London, 1998)

Lyons, F.S.L. *Ireland Since the Famine* (London, 1971)

McBride, I. *The Siege of Derry in Ulster Protestant Mythology* (Dublin, 1998)

McCartney, D. *Parnell: The Politics of Power* (Dublin, 1991)

MacDonagh, O. *States of Mind: A Study of Anglo-Irish Conflict, 1780–1980* (London, 1983)

McNally, P. *Parties, Patriots and Undertakers: Parliamentary Politics in Early Hanoverian Ireland* (Dublin, 1997)

Maguire, W. (ed.) *Kings in Conflict: The Revolutionary War in Ireland and its Aftermath, 1689–1750* (Belfast, 1990)

Mallie, E. and D. McKittrick. *The Fight for Peace: The Secret Story Behind the Irish Peace Process* (London, 1996)

Miller, K.A. *Emigrants and Exiles: Ireland and the Irish Exodus to North America* (Oxford, 1995)

O'Connor, E. *A Labour History of Ireland, 1841–1960* (Dublin, 1992)

O'Day, A. *Irish Home Rule, 1867–1921* (Manchester, 1998)

Ó Gráda, C. *Ireland: A New Economic History, 1780–1939* (Oxford, 1994)

O'Toole, F. *The Ex-Isle of Erin* (Dublin, 1997)

Ó Tuathaigh, G. *Ireland Before the Famine: 1798–1848* (Dublin, 1990)

Purdie, B. *Politics in the Streets: The Origins of the Civil Rights Movement in Northern Ireland* (Belfast, 1990)

Smyth, J. *The Men of No Property: Irish Radicals and Popular Politics in the Late Eighteenth Century* (Dublin, 1992)

Stewart, A.T.Q. *The Summer Soldiers: The 1798 Rebellion in Antrim and Down* (Belfast, 1995)

Ward, M. *Unmanageable Revolutionaries: Women and Irish Nationalism* (London, 1995)

Whelan, K. *The Tree of Liberty: Radicalism, Catholicism and the Construction of Irish Identity, 1760–1830* (Cork, 1996)

Whyte, J.H. *Interpreting Northern Ireland* (Oxford, 1990)

Wichert, S. *Northern Ireland Since 1945* (London, 1999)

INDEX